ROBERT BORY LUDWIG VAN BEETHOVEN

ROBERT BORY

Ludwig van Beethoven

His Life and his Work in Pictures

ATLANTIS BOOKS ZURICH — NEW YORK

TRANSLATED FROM THE FRENCH BY WINIFRED GLASS AND HANS ROSENWALD

LUDWIG VAN BEETHOVEN (1823)
Painting by Ferdinand Waldmüller

The painting was commissioned by Breitkopf & Härtel, Leipzig. Having allowed the painter but one session, Beethoven made such difficulties for him that Waldmüller decided to complete his work from memory. Did the painter mean to revenge himself on Beethoven or did he just happen to immortalize the expression of an ill-humored Beethoven? (Breitkopf & Härtel Archive)

TRANSLATIONS OF BEETHOVEN'S LETTERS
AND VARIOUS DOCUMENTS REPRODUCED IN THIS VOLUME

Page 41

DEDICATION TO THE KURFÜRST MAXIMILIAN-FRIEDRICH ARCHBISHOP OF COLOGNE, AT BONN (1783)

Most Illustrious Highness!

Since my fourth year music has been the first of my youthful occupations. Thus early acquainted with the gracious art which filled my soul with pure harmonies, I became fond of it, and, as it often appeared to me, it liked me. I have reached my eleventh year; and often has the Muse whispered to me in inspired hours: "Try for once and record the harmonies of thy soul!" Eleven years old—methought—and how would an author's air agree with me? And what would masters of the art say to it? I almost became diffident. Yet my Muse insisted—I obeyed and wrote.

May I now venture, Most Illustrious Prince, to place the first fruit of my youthful work at your throne? And may I venture to hope that you will bestow on it the benevolent paternal look of your encouraging approval? Oh yes! the arts and sciences have always found a wise protector in you, a generous patron, and budding talent has prospered under your noble fatherly care.—

Full of this encouraging assurance, I venture to approach Your Most Serene Highness with these youthful attempts. Accept them as a pure offering of the homage paid by a child, and look graciously on them and on their young author.

Ludwig van Beethoven

Page 55

LETTER OF BEETHOVEN TO COUNCILLOR VON SCHADEN, AT AUGSBURG

The 15th of October, Bonn 1787

My noble, aristocratic and specially worthy Friend,

I can easily imagine what you think of me; and I cannot deny that you have good cause for not entertaining a good opinion of me. In spite of that, I will not offer excuses and instead show the reasons and hope that my excuses will be accepted on their grounds. I must acknowledge that since I left Augsburg, my happiness and with it my health began to fail; the closer I came to my native city, the more frequent were the letters from my father asking me to travel faster than I would have done under ordinary circumstances, as my mother's state of health was far from satisfactory. I hurried as fast as I could, even though I myself did not feel well. The desire once more to see my sick mother caused me to remove all obstacles and helped me overcome the greatest difficulties. I found my mother still alive, but in the worst possible state; she was dying of consumption, and the end came about seven weeks ago after she had endured much pain and suffering. She was to me such a good, lovable mother, my best friend. Oh! who was happier than I, when I could still utter the sweet name of mother, and heed was paid to it; and to whom can I say it now?—to the silent pictures resembling her, creations of

my imagination! Since returning here I have enjoyed only a few pleasant hours; during the whole time I have been troubled by asthma, and I much fear that it will lead to consumption. I also suffer from melancholy—for me almost as great an evil as is my illness. Imagine yourself now in my place, and I hope that you will forgive my long silence. As you showed extraordinary kindness and friendship at Augsburg in lending me three carolins, I must beg of you to be still patient with me. My journey was expensive, and here I have not the slightest hope of earning anything. Fate has not been good to me here in Bonn. Please excuse my having detained you so long with my prattling, but everything was necessary to apologize to you. I hope you will not refuse further to extend your honored friendship to me; I have no greater desire than to prove myself worthy of it to some degree. I am, with all respect,

Your most obedient servant and friend,

L. v. Beethoven
Court Organist

Page 91

BEETHOVEN'S LETTER TO HIS FRIEND CARL AMENDA

Vienna, July 2, (1801?)

My dear, my good Amenda, my warm-hearted Friend,

I received and read your last letter with deep emotion, and with a mixture of pain and pleasure. To what can I compare your fidelity and devotion to me? Ah! it is indeed delightful that you still continue to be so good to me. I know you are a proven friend and happily, not like a Viennese friend. No! you are one of those whom the soil of my fatherland Germany produces: how often I wish that you were with me, for your Beethoven is very unhappy. You must know that one of my precious faculties, my hearing, is becoming very defective; even while you were still with me I felt indications of this, though I said nothing, but now it is much worse. Whether I shall ever be cured remains yet to be seen: it is supposed to have its origin in the intestines, but I am almost entirely recovered in that respect. I hope indeed that my hearing may also improve, yet I dare scarcely think so, for attacks of this kind are considered incurable. How sad my life must now be!—forced to shun all that is most dear and precious to me, and to live with such miserable egotists as Zmeskall, Schuppanzigh, etc. Of all my friends Lichnowsky is the only genuine. Beginning last year he granted me a six hundred florins income, which, together with the receipts from my works, enables me to live free from care as to my daily maintenance. All that I now write I could dispose of five times over and be well paid for it. I have been writing a good deal latterly, and as I hear that you have ordered some pianos from . . ., I will send you a lot of things in the case of one of these instruments. In that manner they will not cost you so much.

To my great comfort, a person has returned here whose company I enjoy as well as his disinterested friendship, one of the friends of my youth. I have often spoken to him of you, and told him that since I left my fatherland, you are one of those to whom my heart specially clings. Z. does not quite please him; he is, and always will be, too weak for a true friendship, and I look on him and—as mere instruments on which I play when I please, but never can they grow into noble witnesses of my inner and overt actions, or feel true sympathy for me: I value them only to the extent which their service deserves. Oh! how happy should I now be, had I my full sense of hearing; I would then hasten to you, whereas as it is, I must withdraw from everything. My best years will thus pass without my being able to realize all that my talents and powers have enabled me to execute. In melancholy and resignation I take refuge! I had decided to rise above all this, but how is it possible? If in the course of six months my malady be pronounced incurable, then, Amenda! I shall appeal to you to leave all else and come to me. When I travel (my affliction is less distressing when I play and compose, and most so in my relations with others), you must be my companion. I have the feeling that the good fortune will not forsake me, for what is it to which I could aspire? Since you were here I have written everything except operas and church music. You will not, I know, refuse my plea; you will help your friend to bear his burden and calamity. I have also very much perfected my pianoforte playing, and I hope that a concert tour would possibly contribute to your own success in life, and you would thenceforth always remain with me. I duly received all your letters, and though I did not reply to them, you were constantly on my mind, and my heart beats for you as tenderly as ever. I beg you to keep the fact concerning my hearing a profound secret, and not discuss it with anybody. Write to me frequently: your letters, however short, console and cheer me up, so I shall soon hope to hear from you.

Do not let anyone play your quartet (opus 18, No. 1), as I have altered it very much, having only now succeeded in writing quartets properly: this you will at once understand when you receive it. Now, farewell, my dear kind friend! If by any chance I can serve you here in any way at all, I need not say that you have only to say so and order

your faithful and truly attached

L. v. Beethoven

Page 97

BEETHOVEN'S NOTE TO STEPHAN VON BREUNING

My dear and much loved Stephan,

May our temporary estrangement be forever effaced by the portrait I now send. I know that I have hurt you. The unrest of my heart which you cannot fail to see in me has sufficiently punished me for everything. There was no malice towards you, for then I should be no longer worthy of your friendship. It was passion of friendship both on your part and on mine; but mistrust was rife within me, for people had come between us, unworthy both of you and of me.

My portrait was long ago intended for you; you knew that it was destined for someone—and to whom could I give it with such warmth of heart, as to you, my faithful, good, and noble Stephan?

Forgive me for having grieved you, but I did not suffer any less than did you when I no longer saw you near me. I then first keenly felt how dear you were, and ever will be to my heart. Surely you will once more embrace me as you formerly did.

Yours . . .

Pages 102 and 103

SO-CALLED HEILIGENSTADT TESTAMENT (1802)

TO MY BROTHERS KARL AND (JOHANN) BEETHOVEN

Oh! ye who think or declare me to be hostile, morose, and misanthropical, how unjust you are, and how little you know the secret cause of what appears thus to you! My heart and mind were ever from childhood inclined to the most tender feelings of affection, and I was always disposed to accomplish something great. But you must remember that six years ago I was attacked by an incurable malady, aggravated by incapable physicians, deluded from year to year, too, by the hope of relief, and at length forced to the conviction of a lasting affliction (the cure of which may go on for years, and perhaps after all prove futile).

Born with a passionate and excitable temperament, keenly susceptible to the pleasures of society, I was yet obliged early in life to isolate myself, and to pass my existence in solitude. If I at any time resolved to surmount all this, oh! how cruelly was I again repelled by the experience, sadder than ever, of my defective hearing!—and yet I found it impossible to say to others: Speak louder, shout! for I am deaf! Alas! How could I proclaim the deficiency of a sense which ought to have been more perfect with me than with other men— a sense which I once possessed in the highest perfection, to an extent, indeed, that few in my profession ever enjoyed! Alas! I cannot do this! Forgive me therefore when you see me withdraw from you with whom I would so gladly mingle. My misfortune is doubly severe from causing me to be misunderstood. No longer can I enjoy recreation in social intercourse, refined conversation, or mutual outpourings of thought. Completely isolated, I only enter society when compelled to do so. I must live like an exile. In company I am assailed by the most painful apprehensions, from the dread of being exposed to the risk of my condition being observed. It was the same during the last six months I spent in the country. My intelligent physician recommended me to spare my hearing as much as possible, which was quite in accordance with my present disposition, though sometimes, tempted by my natural inclination for society, I allowed myself to be beguiled into it. But what humiliation when anyone beside me heard a flute in the far distance, while I heard nothing, or when others heard a shepherd singing, and I still heard nothing! Such things brought me to the verge of desperation, and well nigh caused me to put an end to my life. Art! art alone deterred me. Ah! how could I possibly quit the world before bringing forth all that I felt it was my vocation to produce? And thus I spared this miserable life—so utterly miserable that any sudden change may reduce me at any moment from my best condition into the worst. It is decreed that I must now choose Patience for my guide! This I have done. I hope the resolve will not fail me so I can steadfastly persevere till it may please the inexorable Fates to cut the thread of my life. Perhaps I may get better, perhaps not. I am prepared for either. Constrained to become a philosopher in my twenty-eighth year! This is no slight trial, and more severe on an artist than on anyone else. God looks into my heart, he searches it, and knows that love for man and feelings of benevolence have their abode there! Oh! ye who may one day read this, think that you have done me injustice, and let anyone similarly afflicted be consoled, by finding one like himself, who, in defiance of all the obstacles of nature, has done all in his power to be included in the ranks of estimable artists and men. My brothers Karl and Johann, as soon as I am no more, if Professor Schmidt be still alive, beg him in my name to describe my malady, and to add these pages to the analysis of my disease, that at least, so far as possible, the world may be reconciled to me after my death. I also hereby declare you both heirs of my small fortune (if so it may be called). Share it fairly, agree together and assist each other. You know that anything you did to give me pain has been long forgiven. I thank you, my brother Karl in particular, for the attachment you have shown me of late. My wish is that you may enjoy a happier life, and one more free from care, than mine has been. Recommend Virtue to your children; that alone, and not wealth, can ensure happiness. I speak from experience. It was Virtue alone which sustained me in my misery; I have to thank her and Art for not having ended my life by suicide. Farewell! Love each other. I gratefully thank all my friends, especially Prince Lichnowsky and Professor Schmidt. I wish one of you to keep Prince Lichnowsky's instruments; but I trust this will give rise to no dissension between you. If you think it more beneficial, however, you have only to dispose of them. How much I shall rejoice if I can serve you even in the grave! So be it then! I joyfully hasten to meet Death. If he comes before I have had the opportunity of developing all my artistic powers, then, notwithstanding my cruel fate, he will come too early for me, and I should wish for him at a more distant period; but even then I shall be content, for his advent will release me from a state of endless suffering. Come when he may, I shall meet him with courage. Farewell! Do not forget me, even in death: I deserve this from you, because during my life I so often thought of you, and wished to make you happy. Amen!

Heiligenstadt, October 6, 1802,

Ludwig van Beethoven

Heiligenstadt, October 10. Thus, then, I take leave of you, and with sadness too. The fond hope I brought with me here, of being to a certain degree cured, now utterly forsakes me. As autumn leaves fall and wither, so are my hopes blighted. Almost as I came, I depart. Even the lofty courage that so often animated me in the lovely days of summer is gone forever. Oh, Providence! vouchsafe me one day of pure felicity! How long have I been estranged from the glad echo of true joy! When! oh, my God! when shall I again feel it in the temple of nature and of man?—never? Ah! that would be too hard!

BEETHOVEN'S LETTER TO THE "IMMORTAL BELOVED"

July 6, (1812) in the morning

My angel, my all, my very self—only a few words today and at that with pencil (with yours)—not till to-morrow will my lodgings be definitely determined upon—what a useless waste of time for such things. Why this deep sorrow where necessity speaks—can our love exist except through sacrifices—except through not demanding everything—can you change it that you are not wholly mine, I not wholly thine. Oh, God! look out into the beauties of nature and calm your soul for that which must be—love demands everything and that very justly—thus it is for me with you, and for you with me—only you forget so easily that I must live for me and for you. If we were wholly united, you would feel the pain of it as little as I. My journey was a fearful one; I did not reach here until 4 o'clock yesterday morning; lacking horses the post-coach chose another route—but what an awful one. At the stage before the last I was warned not to travel at night—made fearful of a forest, but that only made me the more eager and I was wrong; the coach broke down on the wretched road, a bottomless, mere country-road—without such postilions as I had with me, I should have stuck in the road. Esterhazy, travelling the usual road hitherward, had the same fate with eight horses that I had with four—yet I got some pleasure out of it, as I always do when I successfully overcome difficulties. Now a quick change to things internal from things external. We shall soon, I fancy, see each other; even today I cannot communicate to you the observations I have made during the last few days touching my own life—if our hearts were always close together I would make none of the kind. My heart is full of many things to say to you—Ah!—there are moments when I feel that speech is nothing at all—cheer up—remain my true, my only treasure, my all as I am yours; the gods must send us the rest, that which must and shall be for us.

Your faithful   Ludwig

Evening, Monday, July 6

You are suffering, my dearest creature—only now have I learned that letters must be posted very early in the morning Mondays, Thursdays,—the only days on which the mail-coach goes from here to K. You are suffering—Ah! wherever I am there you are also, and I am with you. I shall arrange affairs so that I may live with you, what a life!!! thus!!! Thus without you—pursued by the goodness of mankind here and there—which I as little try to deserve as I deserve it. Humility of man towards man—it pains me—and when I consider myself in connection with the universe, what am I and what is he whom we call the Greatest—and yet—herein lies the divine in man. I weep when I reflect that you will probably not receive the first intelligence from me until Saturday—much as you love me, I love you more—but do not ever conceal your thoughts from me—good-night—as I am taking the baths, I must go to bed. Oh, God! so near so far! Is our love not truly a celestial edifice—but also firm as Heaven's vault.

Good morning, on July 7

Though still in bed my thoughts go out to you, my Immortal Beloved, now and then joyfully, then sadly, waiting to learn whether or not fate will hear us. I can live only wholly with you or not at all—yes, I am resolved to wander far away so long until I can fly to your arms and say that I am really at home, send my soul enwrapped in you into the land of spirits. Yes, unhappily it must be so—you will be the more resolved since you know my fidelity to you—no one can ever again possess my heart—none—never—Oh, God, why is it necessary to part from one whom one so loves and yet my life in V. (Vienna) is as now a wretched life—your love made me both the happiest and the unhappiest of men—at my age I need a steady, quiet life—can that be under our relations? My angel, I have just been told that the mail-coach goes every day—therefore, I must close at once so that you may receive the L. at once. Be calm, only by a calm consideration of our existence can we achieve our purpose to live together—be calm—love me—today—yesterday—what tearful longings for you—you—you—my life—my all—farewell—Oh, continue to love me—never misjudge the most faithful heart of your beloved L.

ever thine
ever mine
ever for each other

PLEA SENT BEETHOVEN BY VIENNESE MUSIC-LOVERS (February, 1804)

TO MR. LUDWIG VAN BEETHOVEN

Among the numerous of your art who live in the city of your choice and pay homage and admiration to your genius, we who are some of these friends of yours, are hereby taking the liberty and address to you a request harbored by us for a long time.

Even though we are but a small minority who have recognized the value of your work and the tranquillity of mind which these works will exude in future times, we dare to make ourselves the advocates of your admirers who are in number many times our own. The undersigned for whom the realization of an artistic idea is significant and much more important than just an object of pastime, firmly believe that their wishes are equally the wishes, expressed or never articulated, of all those who understand the divine mission of music. Above all the desires we here formulate today are those of your compatriots because the name of Beethoven and his creations, even though belonging as they do to the entire world and to every country where music is cultivated, are associated with Austria which for several reasons has a right to consider you as one of her sons.

The Austrians have great memories of the immortal masterworks which Haydn and Mozart created on Austrian soil. They realize with pride that an élite uniting their two names with yours is a vibrant symbol of sovereignty in the world of music which is in the very care of their fatherland.

It is therefore with sorrow that they have witnessed a strange and foreign esthetics of art finding its refuge here—right close to the graves of the two masters who have passed and in the face of the surviving third of this musical trinity. They know that this new spirit has nothing that would reconcile it with the vision of the great masters, for poverty of inspiration is its mark and with lack of dignity the true sense of a moral beauty is rapidly decreasing and disappearing.

More than ever they are aware that an effort must be made so that a new manifestation of your genius is necessary. In the name of all friends of the arts in this country it is for this reason that we today are sending this plea to you begging you no longer to delay the performance of your most recent masterworks. We have learned that a great work of religious music has been created by you in which you immortalize the feelings of a soul transfigured by the power of fidelity and divine light. We are not unconscious of the fact that equally a new star is shining in the midst of your marvelous symphonies. For years now, ever since the "Battle of Vittoria," have we been expecting impatiently your return so that these new works of yours would be heard by your friends. Please do not disappoint this general expectation any longer and conduct these works, you yourself, in their first performances. Please do not permit under any circumstances that your recent creations could in the future be considered, in the very homeland, as foreign by such people to whom your inspiration has remained unknown. Give us the pleasure to allow us to find you again and to be your admirers. That is our most ardent plea and our first concern.

Other pleas and requests have likewise been made to you. More than a year ago both the management of the Royal Opera and the Austrian Society of Friends of Music were admirers of your art but their solicitations have remained mute for too long a time and have awakened too much hope for everyone, the more so since they were not met with vivid sympathy.

Poetry has made contribution to the intensification of hopes and wishes. A departure of a master as respected and beloved as you are would refuse nourishment to the hopes they have harbored. You should not refuse these pressing invitations which have as their object so noble a goal. May you not delay those days where the chance of Polyhymnia will seize the disciples of music and the heart of every citizen.

May we tell you how much your isolation has caused us regret? Is it necessary to assure you how your friends have deplored that you, the man who is the most gifted among contemporary composers, had to accept without a word the fact that a foreign art had taken possession of the place of honor reserved for the German muse? What shame that these works of national significance had to find themselves relegated to secondary importance so that foreign arias and a new fashion came along to replace the golden age of music in the very country in which the noblest artists lived and worked. You alone can make a decisive victory of our efforts assured. It depends upon you if the Society of National Art and the Opera can hope for a new blossoming period and a new victory of truth and beauty over violence, a victory to which the present fashion must subject itself as to the eternal laws of music. Give us hope that we might see the wishes of all those realized who at all times have been the admirers of your music. That is our second immediate plea.

Do not allow the year which has just begun to run out without having brought us the fruits of these pleas and may the coming spring bring to all friends of music a two-fold flowering.

Vienna, in February, 1824

Prince E. Lichnowsky	Ferdinand Count Palffy	Moritz Count von
Artaria & Cie	Ed. Baron von Schweiger	Dietrichstein
von Hauschka	Count Czernin	J. G. Ritter von Mosel
M. J. Leidersdorf	Moritz Count von Fries	Carl Czerny
J. E. von Wayna	J. F. Castelli	Moritz Count Lichnowsky
Andreas Streicher	Prof. Deinhardtstein	Zmeskall
Anton Halm	Ch. Kuffner	Court Councillor Kiesewetter
Abbé Stadler	F. R. Nehammer	Leopold Sonnleithner
von Felsburg	Steiner von Felsburg	S. A. Steiner & Cie
Ferdinand Count		Anton Diabelli
von Stockhammer		J. N. Bihler

Page 212

LETTER-TESTAMENT ADDRESSED BY BEETHOVEN TO DR. BACH

Vienna, Wednesday, January 3, 1827

My respected friend,

I hereby declare, at my decease, my beloved nephew, Karl van Beethoven, sole heir of all my property, and of seven Bank shares in particular, as well as any ready money I may be possessed of. If the law prescribes any modifications in this matter, pray endeavor to regulate these as much as possible to his advantage.

I appoint you his curator, and beg that, together with Hofrath Breuning, his guardian, you will supply the place of a father to him.

God bless you! A thousand thanks for all the love and friendship you have shown towards me.

Ludwig van Beethoven

Page 212

BEETHOVEN'S LETTER TO BARON JOHN-BAPTIST PASQUALATI
(March 14, 1827)

My esteemed Friend,

Many thanks for the dish you sent me yesterday, which will suffice for today also. I am allowed to have game; and the doctor said that fieldfares were very wholesome for me. I only tell you this for information, as I do not want them today. Forgive this stupid note, but I am exhausted from a sleepless night. I embrace you, and am, with much esteem, your attached friend

(L. van Beethoven)

Page 213

CONTRACT BETWEEN BEETHOVEN AND THE FIRM OF SCHOTT AND SONS, AT MAINZ

DECLARATION

According to which I hand over to the publishing firm of B. Schott the sole copyright of my last Quartet in C sharp minor as well as the sole right of performance. And, further, they are free to print and publish, as their own property in Paris as well as in Mainz and also at all places, the abovementioned firm may think proper.

Vienna, March 20, 1827

Stephan de Breuning
as designated witness.

Ludwig van Beethoven
Ant. Schindler
Director of music, in
the capacity of designated
witness

Page 213

LAST TESTAMENT OF BEETHOVEN

I appoint my nephew Karl my sole heir. The capital of my bequest, however, to devolve on his natural or testamentary heirs.

Lu(d)wig van Beethoven

Preface

THE book which I present to the public herewith is part of a series of iconographies which I have been editing for more than twenty years. They are concerned with the great masters of music.

Just as the preceding works such as "The Life of Franz Liszt in Pictures", "Life and Work of Richard Wagner in Pictures", "Life and Work of W. A. Mozart in Pictures", and "Life of Chopin in Pictures" began with a brief biographical survey, so does this book, the fifth of the series. The survey serves as a guide to those wishing to study the 200 pages of documents compiled here. My labor consisted chiefly of the collection of the approximately 550 portraits, engravings and documents of various sorts. Their juxtaposition in one volume reflects the agitated and tragic life of Beethoven, from his birth in Bonn, in 1770, to his demise in Vienna fifty-seven years later.

This important pictorial material is ordered chronologically. The reproductions carry commentaries. The biography achieved by such a compilation is divided into chapters with titles and subtitles corresponding to the chief periods of the composer's life.

Of the portraits of Beethoven and members of his family, those whose authenticity is doubtful are eliminated. This holds true particularly for the apocryphal portraits of his parents and for the miniature supposedly representing Ludwig van Beethoven and ascribed to the painter Gerhard Kügelgen. Furthermore, I have confined the material to the portraits created during the composer's lifetime or signed by artists who knew the master personally. Therefore one should not look for any of those innumerable pictures, medals or sculptures made long after his death. On the other hand, despite patient research I did not always succeed in obtaining the portraits of relatives, friends or interpreters whose inclusion would have been interesting. I am referring principally to Karl van Beethoven, the master's brother, Zmeskall, his faithful friend, and several others. Yet I was fortunate enough to rediscover a portrait of the violinist Karl Holz who for a while was Beethoven's closest friend replacing Schindler. To this day this portrait has remained practically unknown.

As concerns the various dwellings of Beethoven in Vienna and its environs, I have incorporated reproductions of the pictures made in Beethoven's time only. Unfortunately, but a few are extant which have captured the familiar places that Beethoven filled with his spirit. Notwithstanding—in order to preserve the character of historical documentation—I discarded the idea of adding modern photographs and reproductions, and refer those interested to the work of Bertha Koch entitled "Beethovenstätten in Wien und Umgebung".

One exception from this rule seemed to be in order: it concerns the house in Bonn in which Beethoven was born; such a picture has to be included in this book in view of the fact that neither painting nor drawing exists which would show it as of the end of the eighteenth century.

O F the numerous problems with which the author of this book was confronted, one of the most delicate to resolve was the question posed by Beethoven's astounding handwriting. The reading of certain letters and of his conversation books is extremely difficult even for people well acquainted with the German language. Was the author to deprive his readers of a great number of reproductions of documents written by the master himself, handwritten documents the very sight of which would afford the reader most touching revelations? We arrived at a solution that seemed satisfactory. On some separate pages an English translation of these documents from Beethoven's hand is provided which the reader can place vis-à-vis the reproductions he finds on the pages of the album.

During my work another problem—this one of purely historical nature—attracted my attention. Everybody knows that for more than a century several well known musicologists have tried to determine to whom the famous letter to the "Immortal Beloved", a moving document of ten pages filled with glowing passion, was addressed. It was found among Beethoven's papers after his death.

Schindler, Beethoven's close friend and first biographer, daringly contended no other than the Countess Guicciardi could be addressed. Her parents stubbornly had opposed her marriage to the composer. Theodor von Frimmel chose the singer Magdalena Wildmann, the American Alexander Wheelock Thayer, Therese von Brunswick; Madame La Mara, on the other hand, believed the "Immortal" to have been Josephine, Therese's sister. With less justification other researches suggested Bettina Brentano, Goethe's famous young friend, or the beautiful Therese Malfatti and the singer Amalie Sebald. All these conjectures gradually proved untenable. Consequently, the French scholar Prod'homme a few years ago could state at the end of a well documented essay on the enigma of the "Immortal Beloved": "One must forget the desire to unveil the secret surrounding this 'Immortal Beloved', this creature comparable to an angel transfigured by the glowing phantasy of her lover and to whom Beethoven rushed that rainy summer day of 1812 through the Bohemian forest... History and scholarship are silent and obstinate and fail to give us the key to this mystery but keep her name a secret so that it will remain unknown."

However, repeated defeats did not discourage new investigations. An Israeli author, Siegmund Kasnelson, published a book of 450 pages in 1954 supposedly proving once and forever that Josephine von Brunswick, whose name was first Countess Deym, later Baroness von Stackelberg, was Beethoven's "Immortal Beloved", as La Mara had contended. Beyond that, Kasnelson even believed he had proof that Beethoven was the father of the Baroness' last child, the little Minona von Stackelberg, born April 8, 1813. Professor Dr. Joseph Schmidt-Görg, director of the Beethoven Archive and of the Beethoven House in Bonn, answered, in August, 1957, these sensational claims by publishing "Thirteen Unknown Letters of Beethoven to Josephine Countess Deym née Brunswick" («Dreizehn unbekannte Briefe Beethovens an Josephine Gräfin Deym geb. Brunswick») which had recently been received in the collection supervised by him. He declared Kasnelson's "revelations" untenable.

This verdict was made by so competent an authority that it cannot be contradicted!

My research on the one hand was facilitated to a large extent by the indefatigable cooperation of my collaborators (of whom I shall speak later in this introduction), yet, on the other hand, it was made extraordinarily difficult due to the consequences of the last war. It is generally known that the former Preussische Staatsbibliothek in Berlin (Prussian State Library) owned the majority of Beethoven's autographs and manuscripts. Those responsible for the conservation of these important treasures had distributed them, for safety reasons, to various places so as to prevent destruction through bombing as much as possible. After the occupation of Germany by the foreign armies and the division into two completely different zones it was relatively easy to compile and order those manuscripts and autographs kept in West Germany. However, there were numerous manuscripts and autographs hidden in East Germany during the war which had fallen into unknown hands and had disappeared. Even today the management of the new Deutsche Staatsbibliothek which in East Berlin has replaced the former Preussische Staatsbibliothek, feels compelled to give evasive answers to inquiries pertaining to certain manuscripts.

I have decided to designate as property of the Former State Library in Berlin all documents, autographs and manuscripts which at the beginning of the war, 1939, were in the possession of that institution, hoping that one day all these treasures will be reunited.

To turn to still a different complex of problems: I should like to stress the inestimable service rendered me by the newly published monumental œuvre «Thematisch-Bibliographisches Verzeichnis aller vollendeten Werke Ludwig van Beethovens» ("Thematic-Bibliographical Catalog of all Completed Works of Ludwig van Beethoven") by the eminent musicologist Georg Kinsky, particularly as concerns the difficult questions of first editions of Beethoven's compositions and the dates of their publication. Heretofore researchers in studying these problematical matters had to rely on such outdated works as the «Chronologisches Verzeichnis der Werke Ludwig van Beethovens» ("Chronological Catalog of the Works of Ludwig van Beethoven") published in 1865 by the American Alexander Wheelock Thayer, or «Thematisches Verzeichnis der im Druck erschienenen Werke von Ludwig van Beethoven» ("Thematic Catalog of the Published Works of Ludwig van Beethoven") by Gustav Nottebohm (the second edition of which dates from 1868). Beethoven research in ninety years, however, has made considerable progress so that many corrections of and additions to these old sources became necessary in the course of time.

The work of Kinsky, now available, and to which the author dedicated part of his life without seeing the publication of this, his life's work, is for Beethoven what the last edition of the Köchel Catalog, the work of Einstein, is for Mozart. The care bestowed upon this monumental work, and particularly the new and fastidious numbering system applied for the first time to the works not provided with opus numbers by the master, make Kinsky's research an achievement for which musicians must show humble respect, approval and admiration.

This new system of numbering has been applied here in cases where we treat of a composition of Beethoven which heretofore was not signified by an opus number. In addition, and again leaning on Kinsky's scholarly work, I have corrected the dates of compositions and publications as given by Thayer and Nottebohm where it seemed important. These corrections, in other words, concern dates considered definitive before Kinsky presented the results of his research.

14

AND now I should like to be permitted the discharge of a pleasant duty: to express my gratitude to my principal collaborators who made my investigations easier and who gave of their best to be of assistance to me.

First I must mention Dr. Hans Carl Bodmer of Zürich, recently deceased, the trailblazer of this book. He received me several times with utmost cordiality in his beautiful residence at the Bärengasse where he collected with the most admirable patience and infallible knowledge autographs, manuscripts, portraits and souvenirs of the master of Bonn. It is the most beautiful collection ever owned by a private individual. He generously put his incredible treasures at my disposal and permitted my photographing and reproducing everything I desired, including objects never published and still completely unknown. With greatest interest he followed my investigations, was happy with my discoveries and impatiently anticipated the publication of this book. Unfortunately he was not to see the results of my labor, and his premature death throws a shadow over this work. Further, I should like to thank another generous collector, Mr. Antony van Hoboken of Ascona, who once more opened his extraordinary library of first editions of music and permitted my browsing among his treasures.

The meanwhile deceased Gerhard Wegeler of Koblenz, Mrs. Erna Wegeler of Garmisch-Partenkirchen–both descendants of Beethoven's intimate friend Franz-Gerhard Wegeler–Baron von Boeselager of Heimerzheim, Baron von Gleichenstein of Lahr, Breisgau, M. Alfred Cortot of Lausanne, and the Messrs. Aloys Mooser and Dr. Willy Tappolet of Geneva have put portraits, personal souvenirs of Beethoven and miscellaneous documents at my disposal.

In Bonn Professor Dr. Schmid-Görg, director of the Beethoven Archive and the Beethoven House and his associates Dr. Dagmar Weise and Dr. E.-A. Balling received me most cordially, as did the directress of the Bonn Municipal Archive, Dr. Ennen, and Dr. Oediger, director of the State Archive Düsseldorf, and Mr. de Roo, director and curator of the Mecheln Archive. The directress of the Archive of the Society of Music in Vienna, Dr. Hedwig Kraus, too, has given me excellent assistance, as have Professor Dr. Josef Gregor, director of the Theatrical Collection of the Austrian National Library and his associates Professor Dr. Hans Pauer, director of Engravings and Portraits, and Professor Dr. Novak, director of the Music Collection. It is an especial honor to assure them of my gratitude.

Dr. Glück, director of the Historical Museum of the City of Vienna and his associate Dr. May, Dr. Mitringer, director of the Municipal Library of Vienna, Dr. Hans Jaeger-Sunstenau, director of the Archive of the City of Vienna, as well as Dr. Luithlen, director of the Ancient Instruments Collection of the Kunsthistorisches Museum of Vienna, have assisted me in my research with maximum cooperation.

Finally, Dr. Cremer, director of the Westdeutsche Bibliothek in Marburg, Dr. Virneisel in Tübingen, director of the depository of the former Prussian State Library of Berlin, M. Fédoroff of the Bibliothèque de l'Opéra de Paris and Dr. Auguste Bouvier, director of the Bibliothèque publique et universitaire in Geneva, as well as Dr. D.-C. Parker of Glasgow have my unadulterated thankfulness.
It is a great pleasure indeed to thank these unselfish colleagues here in print.

Ludwig van Beethoven 1770—1827

Beethoven! Of all the great geniuses produced by humanity none has generated such passionate interest and stimulated again and again such curiosity as has the composer of the "Eroica" and the Ninth Symphony. His life and work ever since his death have been treated of incessantly, beginning with the biographies of his contemporaries, Johann-Alois Schlosser, Franz-Gerhard Wegeler, Ferdinand Ries and mainly Anton Schindler, to the more recent of Emmanuel Buenzod, from the musicological studies of Thayer, Nottebohm, Grove and Colombani to the more or less fictional ones of Edouard Herriot or Emil Ludwig. The biographical sketch with which I begin this book does not claim to add anything new to the knowledge of Beethoven, already extensive. The sole aim of this introduction is to furnish the reader of the documents of the book a few points of departure, or if it is a more appropriate term, a basis of reference which would enable him to correlate the pictorial material reflecting the life of suffering of this great musician with his biography.

"Watch him, this fellow will one day be talked about in the whole world." (Mozart)

IN a poor garret, in the dim light of which the master's bust is to be seen today, Ludwig van Beethoven was born December 16, 1770. He was of Flemish origin, a child and grandchild of musicians. His grandfather–his name was Ludwig–was Court *Kapellmeister* of the *Kurfürst* and Archbishop of Cologne, and his father served the court as one of the musicians.

Biographers have very different opinions on the milieu in which Beethoven was born and grew up. Some, basing theirs on the idyllic picture by the baker Fischer, a neighbor, describe it in lovely colors; others like Romain Rolland see but miserable family affairs, with everything suffering from the violence of a father with a penchant for excellent Rhine wines.

Be that as it may, it appears that alcohol did not becloud Johann van Beethoven to such an extent that he remained oblivious to the obvious musical talent of his son. Very early he had Ludwig learn the rudiments of music. First the Franciscan monks teach him the playing of the organ, then one of his cousins, Rovantini, the severe Pfeiffer and Franz Ries introduce him to piano and violin playing. Above all, Christian Gottlob Neefe, the most important of his teachers, exercises his influence upon him so that at barely twelve young Ludwig becomes his substitute as court organist.

Neefe, an educated musician, an erudite man with philosophical interests, has the great merit of having imparted to his pupil most widely differing ideas and a broad knowledge; first he teaches him theory on the basis of the "Well Tempered Keyboard" of Bach, using examples of Italian and French masters, and also referring to Handel—the purest sources possible. Then he introduces him to the duties of an orchestral musician and teaches him musical literature so that Beethoven becomes a competent viola player and coach. For the future creator of "Fidelio" this later proves to be of considerable significance.

In 1787 Beethoven suffers the loss of his mother. The parental home—two additional sons had been born meanwhile—does not survive this fate for any length of time: the father, with his regrettable addiction to liquor, drowns his sorrow. At that moment, for the first time in Beethoven's life, a number of friends and admirers group around the timid and lonely young man, a circle of the type he was to have around him practically all his life. As the family of the archivist von Breuning, to which his friend Wegeler introduced him, accepts Beethoven, he enters an atmosphere which gives his soul and mind refreshing recreation and considerable enrichment. Through Frau von Breuning whom he later called his guardian angel and who knew how "to keep the insects away from the blossom", he contacts a milieu which furthers his culture and education and at the same time soothes his feelings and stimulates friendship. In this hospitable house of poetry and music cultivated with taste and enthusiasm, the evenings are filled with readings of Klopstock and Schiller by Eleonore (later Frau Wegeler), daughter of the house, and her uncles Lorenz and Philipp, and with incomparable musical delights offered largely by young Ludwig himself. In this atmosphere where the fastidious cultivation of the arts is balanced with refinement of education, Beethoven forms friendships of utmost value for his career. Particularly important is that with the Count von Waldstein to whom he was later to dedicate his piano sonata, op. 53, entitled "l'Aurore". This young aristocrat, eight years the composer's senior but of like taste and persuasion, is not content with donating to Beethoven his first piano and commissioning him to write scores (the best known is «Musik zu einem Ritterballet»), but also, together with Neefe, persuades Beethoven to change his residence from Bonn to Vienna.

Haydn, just returned from a trip through the Rhineland, is astounded that Beethoven had not come previously to Vienna to meet him. Waldstein, not satisfied that he had induced the *Kurfürst* and Archbishop to give Beethoven a furlough and the necessary travelling expenses to pay for a sojourn in a foreign country, beyond that puts very many wonderful contacts to the Viennese aristocracy at his friend's and protégé's disposal. Beethoven, scarcely arrived in the city of the Danube, finds the drawing rooms of the Swietens, Lichnowskys, Fries, Schwarzenbergs and Liechtensteins wide open to him.

Beethoven at the time of his settling in Austria is by no means a beginner. In his luggage he has forty-nine works; of these only twenty-one were published during his lifetime, to be sure. Yet, in his estimation, none would be worthy of being called "opus 1". The new settler in Vienna, despite a career so auspiciously started in Bonn, acts as though his recent past had meant nothing.

Without neglecting the contacts made through introductions proferred him by the *Kurfürst* and Count Waldstein he delights in playing the role—in aristocratic circles—of the unpolished small towner. These traits are evident only in his exterior, however, and in the appearances of the brilliant virtuoso—such as he now is. As a creative artist he is not yet conspicuous. He seeks greater profundity and systematic growth in solitude and introspectiveness.

In the manner with which he projects his own future and the discipline with which he subjects himself to his own plans, the passionate desire for construction, indispensable and essential for the art of the symphonist, is reflected. "Must it be? It must be!" is written later at the beginning of one of his quartets.

Now, in 1792, he commences strict studies in counterpoint and fugue under Albrechtsberger's supervision and completes his compositional education under Salieri and Haydn. He makes his living, a much admired pianist, by giving piano lessons. For several years he leads the life of an extrovert, giving concerts in Vienna and touring even Bohemia and Germany. He accepts an invitation to the court of Berlin where he receives a golden tobacco box from the King of Prussia and forms a friendship with Prince Louis Ferdinand, an excellent musician.

From this period derive works under Haydn's predominant influence. They are the beginning of the "first period". Here belong the Trios, op. 1–dedicated to Prince Lichnowsky–the piano sonatas dedicated to Haydn, and the first two cello sonatas, to name but the better known. Three other works, to be sure of differing value, contribute through their immediate success to making Beethoven a most famous personality and to consolidating his prestige: the Sonata for the piano, op. 13, the "Pathétique", the cantata "Adelaide" on lyrics by Matthisson, and a song whose title hints at a somewhat antiquated romanticism «Seufzer eines Ungeliebten» ("Sigh of One Not Loved"). In reality the «Seufzer» rushes things, for it is unlikely that at that time a serious love or grave disappointments disturb his life with tempestuous onslaught. A few years later Beethoven was to have experience, and thoroughly so, also in that respect.

However, now in 1800–Beethoven is doing famously in Vienna. The pianist whose improvisations never fail to make a great impression receives invitations to the finest salons and from the most prominent society. First vying for his presence in their palatial homes, these aristocrats are fully satisfied only when they have turned over the musical education of their families to this young musician.

Beethoven has every reason to be satisfied with the treatment these rich people of the world accord him despite his simple unpolished appearance and his Republican ideas and attitudes which scarcely make him a «natural» for such adulation. Prince Lichnowsky subscribes to 32 copies of the Trio, op. 1. Furthermore, every chamber music work from Beethoven's pen immediately upon completion is performed in this nobleman's palace where the excellent Schuppanzigh plays quartets with Zmeskall, the violinist Weiss, the cellists Kraft and Linke. In Prince Lobkowitz' palace Beethoven has the opportunity to hear his larger scores performed by an impressive orchestra whenever he wishes.

To hear, to hear . . .! The first shadows arise in this happy life with its future of rich perspectives and hopes. Since 1796 his hearing has begun to deteriorate. For a long time he keeps the secret of growing suffering to himself and reveals it only to his intimate friends, Amenda and Wegeler.

Vexed by torturing fear, he rushes from one specialist to another. But all these medical consultations, all these treatments prove failures: cold and lukewarm baths, oil injections, plaster follow in rapid succession and for a short time nourish the hope for convalescence. They fail to bring comfort, real and permanent. Despair overtakes him, he becomes unsociable, escapes the world, avoids even his greatest admirers, hoping to keep his infirmity which so oppresses him a secret.

And another trial begins to overpower this unhappy man who, on certain days, is already completely desperate: the first great love's sorrow. Of all salons (in which despite his fate he must show himself) he loves best that of the Countess Deym née Brunswick. Named "Pepi" in the circle of her friends, she is a pupil of Beethoven as is her older sister Therese. The ties which bind the musician to these sisters and their brother, Count Franz, are source of a solid friendship and mutual sympathies; but these ties were to precipitate him into a painful, unsuccessful romance. For the time being at least he is not in love with either the intelligent melancholy Therese nor her younger sister, but is irresistibly infatuated with one of their cousins who has come to Marton-Vásár, the Hungarian residence of the Brunswicks: she is the attractive young Countess Giulietta Guicciardi. Conscious of his significance as an artist adored by aristocrats, and deriving therefrom his right to dare everything, Beethoven—and never will we know if and to what degree his feelings were reciprocated—begins to dream of marriage and without qualm asks for the hand of the beautiful Countess.

Would he have been happy with this lovable but coquettish, superficial child? One doubts it. The rejection by her parents nevertheless is painful to him beyond belief and when, two years later, the young lady to whom Beethoven dedicates the "Moonlight" sonata marries the Count Gallenberg, the composer exclaims: "There are horrible periods in life which one must survive." Even after two years the wound is not completely healed.

Even more telling of the situation in which Beethoven is during this dark period, and more principally significant and grave, is the document generally known as the "Testament". It is written at the beginning of October 1802 in Heiligenstadt near Vienna. In this attractive hamlet he seeks the refuge befitting his melancholy and feeling of isolation. In the famous letter to his brothers Beethoven reveals his total hopelessness from the utmost consequences of which only his morality protects him.

However, just because of these gruesome experiences and as a result of his being so frequently torn between depression and brief moments of hope, Beethoven's artistry assumes its essential traits in the midst of struggle between sorrow and effort. The piano sonatas op. 26, op. 27, 1 and 2, op. 31, 2 and the piano violin sonata op. 47, the "Kreutzer" sonata—each in its own fashion distinctly bears the stamp of the torture from which the Titan suffers, and is a noteworthy document of his mental unrest.

While problems of various kinds thusly accumulate for Beethoven, Napoleon's victories bring French cannons to Vienna. In this agitated air of warfare Beethoven, whose Second Symphony had still exuded a certain optimism, undertakes the composition of his Third, the "Eroica". It is planned full of enthusiasm and admiration for the young Corsican conqueror, a much glorified, practically legendary figure. Yet Beethoven's enthusiasm is replaced with bitter disappointment when Bonaparte becomes Emperor Napoleon I. Now Beethoven can see in him but an ambitious genius–the man whom he had hopefully viewed as a hero of Roman Republican stature. In an attack of uncommon furor he abolishes the dedication of his "Eroica" to Bonaparte and hence this work is to have no other meaning than that of "celebrating the memory of a great man" («composta per festeggiare il sovvenire di un grand'uomo»). In 1821 when Beethoven hears of the death of the French Emperor on St. Helena, his final appraisal of the man is contained in that often-referred-to comment, "I have composed the music suitable to this event seventeen years ago."

Curiously enough, the troubled war years which transform the environs of Vienna into an armored camp and during which the French (to whom Beethoven does not show friendliness) rattled sabers on the Prater coincide with the period in which Beethoven's feelings of love gain musical and dramatic expression in "Fidelio". This work which lays bare the master's innermost sentiments as few others do, is presented on the stage in November 1805 at the Theater an der Wien; it is the day after Austerlitz when it is heard by an audience consisting partly of French military personnel of occupation troops, we would say today.

In spite of the absence of truly dramatic qualities, the Bouilly libretto, following an authentic episode from the persecution period of the French Revolution, is a source of great satisfaction to Beethoven for it provides him with an opportunity to glorify marital love and fidelity.

A FTER the brief and modest success of his sole opera, Beethoven is absorbed, between 1805 and 1808, in working on his C minor Symphony, the Fifth; the two overtures "Leonore" (Nos. 2 and 3) for the opera "Fidelio", and the Fourth Piano Concerto (G major). In addition, the so-called "Appassionata", op. 57, a monumental piano sonata, is born as is the Fourth Symphony.

The latter, a symphony luminous and replete with happy moods, represents an obvious contrast to so many works preceding it, and which are darker and more austere, so that certain biographers recognize therein the strong dualism of the composer and point to it as a reflection of his amorous adventures having its source in his passionate love for Therese von Brunswick and in a secret engagement to her. Here we touch upon a problematical and controversial question the core of which lies in the mystery surrounding the

22

letter to the "Immortal Beloved". Even if the engagement to Therese is probable–her own words would justify the assumption that they were affianced–it is also certain that their plans met with an opposition similar to that which several years before had suddenly ended the musician's romance with Therese's cousin, Giulietta Guicciardi.

Beethoven almost would have left Vienna. A concert of December 22, 1808 given under his own direction is a grave disappointment–the performance of the C minor Symphony, followed by the just completed "Pastorale" and, finally, by the Fantasy for piano, chorus and orchestra, another of his just completed works. The hall is badly heated, the soloists make mistakes, the ensemble performing the Fantasy practically falls apart. Finally when the latter work is repeated all goes wrong again and the entire affair turns out to be a catastrophe. The music lovers of Vienna walk out on him.

At that time, however, King Jerome of Westphalia, Napoleon's brother, makes a most attractive proposition, an annual salary of 600 gold ducats if Beethoven would move to Kassel and conduct several concerts there every season–whereas the remainder of the time would be at Beethoven's disposal for composing. At the instigation of a faithful friend, Countess Erdödy (who upon hearing of the offer alarms Beethoven's Viennese friends), three patrons unite; the Austrian capital is indebted to this triumvirate–she can retain one of the greatest geniuses she has ever given asylum. On March 1, 1809 Archduke Rudolf of Austria, Prince Ferdinand Kinsky and Prince Lobkowitz sign an agreement obligating themselves to the annual payment of 4000 florins to the master. Now Beethoven need not quit Vienna; at least for some years to come his financial situation is assured "in accordance with the personal needs of the composer". The result is an unhampered outpouring, and is particularly evident from 1809 to 1812. This is the period of the Fifth Piano Concerto, the overture and stage music to "Egmont", and especially of the Seventh and Eighth symphonies.

In addition to these orchestral works, the string quartets op. 74 and op. 95 must be mentioned as well as the piano sonata op. 78, so often underestimated, and the marvelous piano sonata op. 81 a, the last movement of which («Wiedersehen») spontaneously celebrates the return of the "beloved Archduke Rudolf to his dear Vienna". To him, Beethoven's treasured patron, «Les Adieux» is dedicated.

Testimonies of close friends such as Wegeler and Zmeskall reveal that during this period Beethoven suddenly indulges in certain luxuries in his wardrobe and household, and they are first to be astounded by such new traits. The reason lies in the fact that now with fewer financial cares he again becomes involved in sentiments of the heart. Baron Gleichenstein, one of his friends, is about to become engaged to Anna Malfatti, a charming young woman. With her sister Therese Beethoven soon falls passionately in love. She is a lovable creature, to be sure, but superficial and irresponsible. The creator of the

"Appassionata", to flatter her, goes as far as to walk her dog. Yet his submissiveness is futile. Therese Malfatti has set her mind on becoming a Baron's wife and Beethoven soon discovers her social ambitions.

Another romance has ended in tragedy. However, Beethoven makes acquaintance with other young ladies so as to heal, more or less, the wounds inflicted by this affair. Among these women the brilliant Bettina Brentano shines most conspicuously but at the same time ambiguously. A young woman of high intelligence she is youthful and yet mature, aggressive, educated, excessive in her passionateness, untiring in her ambitiousness. The role to which she appoints herself in Beethoven's and Goethe's lives leaves a peculiar impression, yet one can scarcely deny that this young woman who (before she married Achim von Arnim) made old Goethe's heart fly higher, was most stimulating for Beethoven. We know very little about the Teplitz meeting of the composer of the "Eroica" and the creator of "Faust". One thing is certain, however: while Beethoven had profound admiration for the famous poet, Goethe, in matters musical following staunchly the ideas of his friend Zelter, regarded Beethoven as a genius, but at the same time as a radical. Beethoven's decisive independence and autonomous conduct displeased the poet. 1813 and 1814 are decisive years in European history: the edifice Napoleon's cannons had built becomes shaky in many sections and the nations he had subjugated one after the other are being liberated. The economic consequences of this general deterioration—the subsequent devaluation of monies—influence Beethoven's financial situation. Despite that fact, and notwithstanding the further decline of his health, the composer makes unselfish efforts to help relatives and friends who are in a situation worse than his own. The many aggravations cannot but hamper his musical productivity. In 1813 his output is relatively meager, and in 1814 he writes casual works such as "Wellington's Victory or the Battle of Vittoria", "Germania's Rebirth", and "The Glorious Moment". The latter work is written in honor of the Congress of Vienna which followed Napoleon's final breakdown. Beethoven's prominent patron Archduke Rudolf affords him the opportunity of meeting the rulers gathered in the Austrian capital. His official appearances and name add to the lustre of the Congress, which in turn heightens his fame but his significance is much more enhanced through the revival of "Fidelio" in a revised form that same year, 1814.

THE remaining twelve years before his death are lacking in important or exciting events. At forty-five, Beethoven, almost a prisoner, retires from the world due to his deafness, now nearly complete. His contact is confined to a few friends whose fidelity is not shaken by the composer's inconsistencies and capriciousness: Breuning, Schindler, Count Moritz Lichnowsky, Countess Erdödy and Archduke Rudolf (who, though remaining in the background, is nevertheless always ready to meet the obstacles of daily living). Beethoven's intellectual and musical energies are now wholly directed towards his inner life.

There is still no end to trials and tribulations! His brother, recently deceased, has left him the guardianship of an undisciplined nephew. The boy is annoyed by the extreme concern of a peculiar uncle and gives Beethoven continuous grave sorrow because of all sorts of stupid pranks. The results are numerous quarrels with an apparently incorrigible good-for-nothing, and then again the sorrow of painful disagreements with the boy's mother, his sister-in-law.

Even though Beethoven has reached the pinnacle of his fame, he nevertheless experiences so much misfortune that his misanthropic tendencies appear intensified. When the "Imperial Director of the Orchestra" passes away, Beethoven fails to succeed to the position and title for which he had hoped. The position remains unfilled.

Should such setbacks matter to one now in the midst of working on gigantic masterworks, the "Missa Solemnis" and the Ninth Symphony, to one who already has completed the two cello sonatas, op. 102, as well as the lofty piano sonatas, op. 101, 106 and 109?

At the same time one must not pass over lightly or ignore the deep financial distress now casting a shadow over the composer's fame. When the Ninth Symphony is performed, the executants, enthusiastic about the work, generously renounce rehearsal fees and say: "All for Beethoven!" Romain Rolland quotes the master as saying that he must give the impression of needing nothing despite his terrible poverty.

Certain satisfactions, however, fill him with pride, such as the cordial reception of the just published "Missa Solemnis" by all the courts of Europe. Louis XVIII, King of France, even adds some flattering remarks to the fifty ducats for a subscription plus a medal with his portrait and the inscription "The King to Monsieur Beethoven".

In the three years after the publication of the Mass and the Ninth, he creates the astonishing "Diabelli Variations" and the five string quartets, perhaps the purest emotions expressed through music.

Just as had Carl Maria von Weber (who died in London the day after an "Oberon" performance a year before) so Beethoven lived the last month of his life in relative relief from monetary concern—thanks to the generosity of the Royal Philharmonic Society. Towards the end of 1826 he stays in the environs of Vienna for several months. He becomes gravely ill. After terrible agonies he succumbs to a complicated pulmonary congestion—according to his physician—on March 26, 1827. It is the result of a cirrhosis of the liver. He passes on while Vienna experiences a sudden spring thunderstorm. Upon a friend of Schubert, Anselm Hüttenbrenner, falls the duty of closing Beethoven's eyes. What irony of fate that Beethoven's belongings, including his great treasure of manuscripts, are auctioned off by court decree! And the price? For 252 books of his music library plus the manuscripts 982 florins and 37 kreutzers were salvaged.

TABLES

VIEW OF MECHELN (1750)
Engraving by August Vind after Jean-Chrétien-Léopold Mechel

The family of Ludwig van Beethoven does not come from Antwerp, as was assumed for some time, but from Mecheln. Since the 17th century they had been in residence there. (Archives of Mecheln)

SAINT-ROMBAUD AT MECHELN
Water color by J. B. de Noter (18th century)

The great-grandparents of Ludwig van Beethoven, Michel van Beethoven and Marie Louise Stuyckers, were married in this church in 1707, and their parents, Corneille van Beethoven and Maria Catharina Leempoel, in 1673. (Archives of Mecheln)

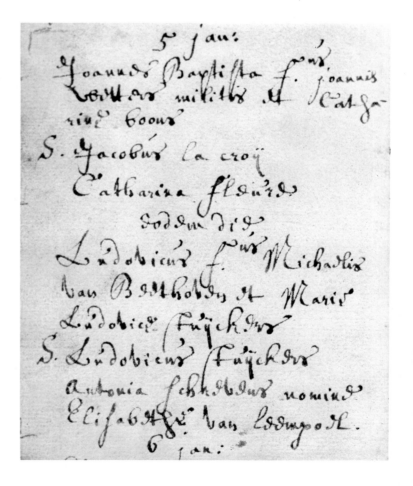

REGISTRY ENTRY OF THE WEDDING OF CORNEILLE VAN
BEETHOVEN TO MARIA CATHARINA LEEMPOEL
(February 12, 1673)

The great-great-grandparents of Ludwig van Beethoven. (Church registry of
Saint-Rombaud; Archives of Mecheln)

REGISTRY ENTRY OF THE CHRISTENING OF
LUDOVICUS VAN BEETHOVEN (January 5, 1712)

Ludwig van Beethoven's grandfather, who left Mecheln and moved to Bonn.
(Church registry of Sainte-Catherine; Archives of Mecheln)

SAINTE-CATHERINE
AT MECHELN
(18th century)

Water color by van den Eynde

Ludovicus van Beethoven,
Ludwig van Beethoven's grand-
father, was christened in this
church on January 5, 1712.
(Church registry of Sainte-
Catherine; Archives of Mecheln)

REGISTRY ENTRY OF THE WEDDING OF MICHEL VAN
BEETHOVEN TO MARIE LOUISE STUYCKERS (October 18, 1707)

Ludwig van Beethoven's great-grandparents. (Church registry of Saint-Rombaud; Archives of Mecheln)

REGISTRY ENTRY OF THE CHRISTENING OF MICHEL VAN
BEETHOVEN (February 15, 1684)

Michel, son of Corneille van Beethoven and Maria Catharina Leempoel, was
Ludwig van Beethoven's great-grandfather. (Church registry of Notre-Dame
at Mecheln; Archives of Mecheln)

THE BEETHOVEN FAMILY SETTLES IN BONN (1733)

In 1733 Ludwig van Beethoven, the grandfather, left Mecheln, and after a short stay at Löwen moved to Bonn, the residence of the Archbishop of Cologne, Kurfürst Clemens August of Bavaria.

THE PALACE AT BONN, RESIDENCE OF THE KURFÜRST OF COLOGNE
From an engraving by Fr. Rousseau

This palace and its priceless interior became a prey to flames in January, 1777. (Municipal Archive, Bonn)

CLEMENS AUGUST OF BAVARIA, KURFÜRST AND ARCHBISHOP OF COLOGNE (1700—1761)
Engraving by G. Bodenehr after A. Vind

Under the reign of this prince of the church Ludwig van Beethoven, the grandfather, settled in Bonn. (Municipal Archive, Bonn)

MAXIMILIAN FRIEDRICH, COUNT VON KÖNIGSEGG-AULENDORF, KURFÜRST AND ARCHBISHOP OF COLOGNE (1708—1784)
Oil painting

He was the successor of Clemens August. (Town Hall, Bonn)

Both rulers, equally fond of splendor and extravagance, endeavored to make their residence Bonn a center of artistic and lavish life, in which the fine arts, the theater and the dance held a more important position than did the church service.

THE PALACE AT BONN

Colored engraving by J. Ziegler after L. Janscha
(Beethovenhaus, Bonn)

MAXIMILIAN FRANZ, KURFÜRST OF COLOGNE (1756—1801)

Engraving by J. E. Mansfeld

Maximilian Franz, the younger brother of Emperor Joseph II, was Archbishop of Cologne from 1784 to 1794, when the troops of the French Revolution expelled him from his diocese. Liberal and highly educated, he protected the arts, especially music and the theater. The young Beethoven enjoyed his particular interest. (National Library, Vienna)

DOCUMENT OF NOMINATION BY CLEMENS AUGUST, KURFÜRST OF COLOGNE (March, 1733)

With this document Ludwig van Beethoven, the grandfather, was appointed to the position of court musician of the Kurfürst. (State Archive, Düsseldorf)

LUDWIG VAN BEETHOVEN, THE GRANDFATHER (1712—1773)

From an oil portrait by A. Radoux

After leaving Mecheln the intelligent and well trained musician settled in Löwen at the age of eighteen. There he began as a tenor at Saint-Pierre and was soon promoted to director of the choir. In 1733 he was called to Bonn as a bass. In 1746 he was given the title of chamber musician of the Archbishop's orchestra. In 1761 he became director of the orchestra. He died in Bonn on December 24, 1773, three years after his grandchild Ludwig was born. (Beethovenhaus, Bonn)

REGISTRY ENTRY OF THE WEDDING OF LUDWIG VAN BEETHOVEN TO MARIA JOSEPHA POLL (September 7, 1733)

(Church registry of St. Remigius; Municipal Archive, Bonn)

Page 9 of the "Kurkölnischer Hofkalender" of 1760

On this page the members of the "Kurfürst's Chamber Orchestra and Court Music" are listed. Among the singers are Ludwig van Beethoven, the grandfather, and his son Johann. (Municipal Archive, Bonn)

Registry entry of the wedding of Johann van Beethoven to Maria Magdalena Keverich (November 12, 1767)

The second child of this marriage was Ludwig van Beethoven, the great composer. (Church registry of St. Remigius; Municipal Archive, Bonn)

Bonn. St. Remigius, in the foreground, with the cemetery

Drawing by W. Schirmer after the engraving by Merian

In this church, which burned in 1801, Ludwig van Beethoven, the grandfather, was married to Maria Josepha Poll in 1733; their son Johann here married Maria Magdalena Keverich in 1767. Their son, the famous Ludwig van Beethoven, was christened here on December 17, 1770. (Municipal Archive, Bonn)

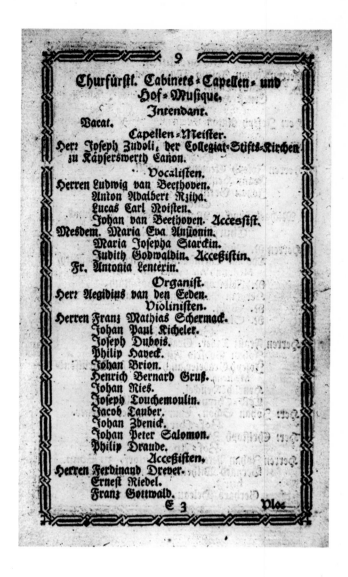

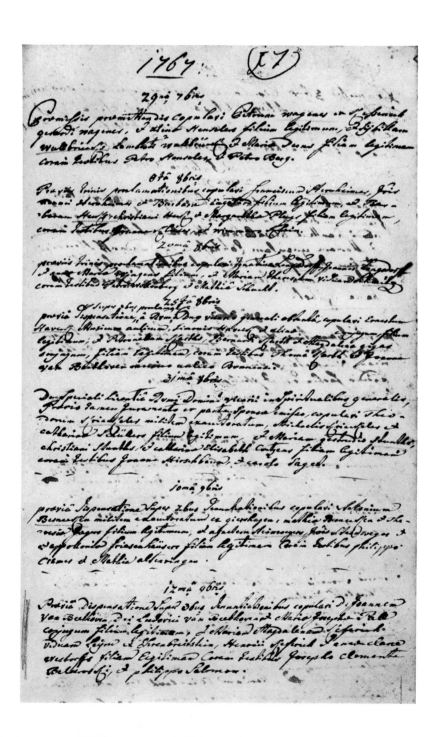

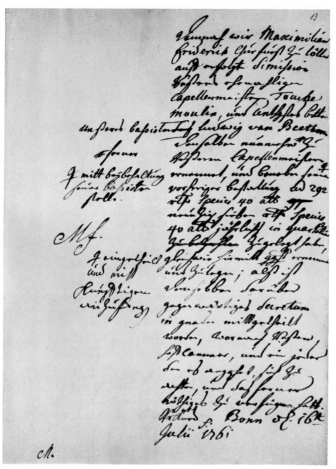

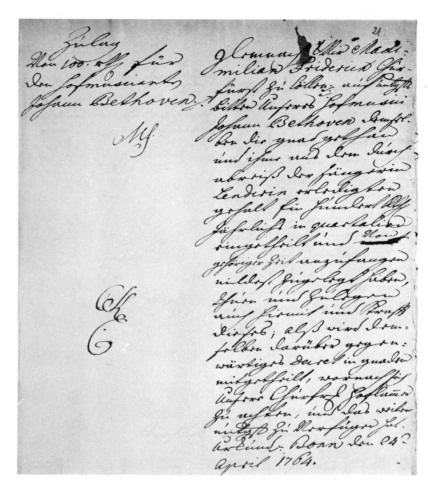

THE ARCHBISHOP'S DOCUMENT OF APPOINTMENT BY WHICH LUDWIG VAN BEETHOVEN, THE GRANDFATHER, WAS PROMOTED TO DIRECTORSHIP OF THE ORCHESTRA (July 16, 1761)

(State Archive, Düsseldorf)

"PAYMENT OF 100 REICHSTHALER TO THE COURT MUSICIAN JOHANN BEETHOVEN" (April 24, 1764)

At the request of his father Ludwig, Johann (who "has already sung the soprano, counter-alto, and tenor voices for 15 years without salary, whenever the necessity occurred, and is also capable of playing the violin") was awarded a modest remuneration, which enabled him to marry three years later. (State Archive, Düsseldorf)

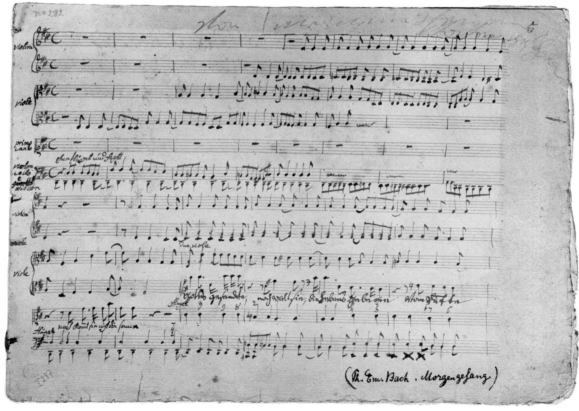

PHILIPP EMANUEL BACH'S "MORGENGESANG" COPIED BY JOHANN VAN BEETHOVEN

This eleven page manuscript is the only known music-autograph by Ludwig van Beethoven's father. Ludwig later made a pencil note at the head of the manuscript: "Written by my dear father." The valuable document was donated to the Beethovenhaus in Bonn by Johannes Brahms in 1893. (Beethovenhaus, Bonn)

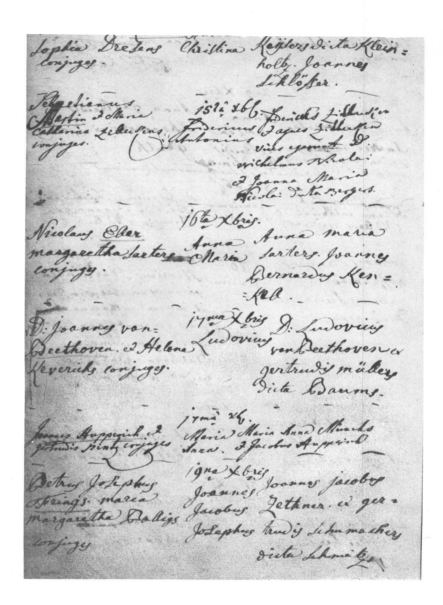

Document of Beethoven's christening
(December 17, 1770)

The composer's mother was erroneously entered as Helena; her name was Magdalena Keverich. Godparents were Ludwig van Beethoven, the grandfather, and Frau Gertrude Baum, a neighbor, owner of the Haus zum Mohren which now houses the Beethoven Archive. (Register of christenings of the Remigius parish, Municipal Archive, Bonn)

Room in which Beethoven was born
The directors of the Beethovenhaus have refrained from repairing and renovating this historic room, and thus have tactfully maintained its solemnity. Only the marble bust by Wolff-Voss has found its place in this shrine.

LUDWIG VAN BEETHOVEN'S CHILDHOOD

THE HOUSE AT No. 934 RHEINGASSE, BONN

Oil painting, not signed

In 1774 the Beethovens left the house at Bonngasse, and in 1776 they moved into the house pictured here. The owner was Fischer, a baker, who with his family inhabited part of the building. The Beethovens lived here until 1787. (Beethovenhaus, Bonn)

THE FISCHER MANUSCRIPT

Gottfried Fischer, son of the baker, chronicled the daily events which concerned the two families. Above all, he reported on the life and experiences of young Ludwig van Beethoven. Thus these notes are of great value for the study of Beethoven's childhood and adolescence. (Beethovenhaus, Bonn)

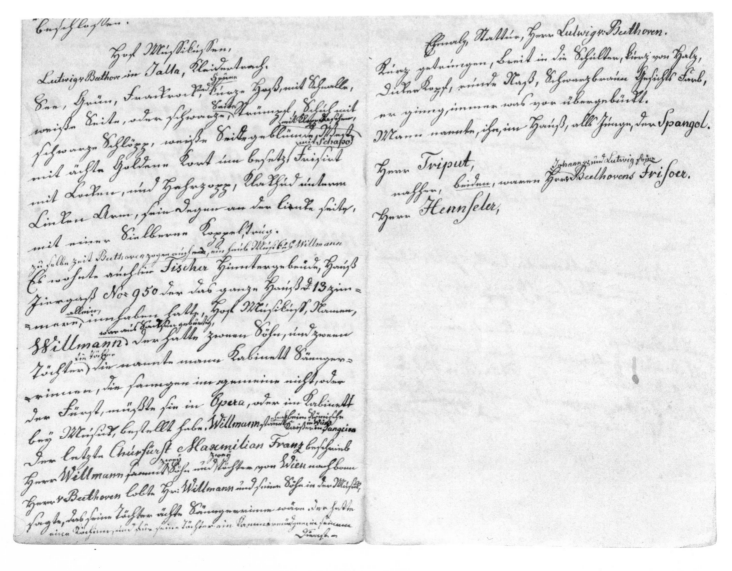

BEETHOVEN'S BIRTHPLACE IN BONN AS IT IS TODAY

Behind the right window in the roof, on the second floor of the modest building, the great master was born. This and the neighboring building, which both face Bonngasse, today house the collections of the Beethovenhaus and the Beethoven Archive.

LUDWIG VAN BEETHOVEN'S MUSICAL EDUCATION

Johann van Beethoven was his son's first music teacher. When he discovered his son's genius, he secured famous musicians then living in Bonn: F. T. Pfeiffer and Rovantini for piano lessons, the organist van den Eeden and the Franciscan monk Willibald Koch, the violinist Franz Ries, and above all, Christian Gottlob Neefe.

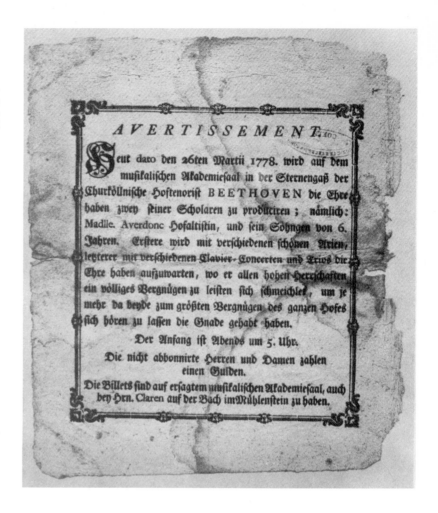

CONCERT ANNOUNCEMENT OF BEETHOVEN'S FIRST PUBLIC APPEARANCE (March 26, 1778)

Like Leopold Mozart, who had his son Wolfgang Amadeus perform for Empress Maria Theresia in Vienna at the age of six, Johann van Beethoven introduced his son Ludwig to the public of the Archbishop's court at the age of seven—not six, as the "Avertissement" incorrectly announces. (Beethovenhaus, Bonn)

CHRISTIAN GOTTLOB NEEFE (1748—1798)
Oil portrait, not signed

Neefe, a distinguished musician and a person of broad education, in 1779 arrived in Bonn as musical director of the National Theater. He became organist of the court and young Beethoven's revered teacher. Beethoven wrote twenty years later: "Should I become a great man you will have had a share in it." (Beethovenhaus, Bonn)

OLD ORGAN AT THE MINORITE MONASTERY IN BONN

When Beethoven was scarcely nine years old he was able to substitute for the monastery's organist. He regularly played the instrument pictured here at early Mass. (Beethovenhaus, Bonn)

AN ARTICLE ON LUDWIG VAN BEETHOVEN,
PUBLISHED IN "C. F. CRAMERS MAGAZIN DER MUSIK"
(March 2, 1787)

The author is Christian Gottlob Neefe. He proves a remarkable prophet.
(Beethovenhaus, Bonn)

Louis van Betthoven, Sohn des obenangeführten Tenoristen, ein Knabe von 11 Jahren, und von vielversprechendem Talent. Er spielt sehr fertig und mit Kraft das Clavier, ließt sehr gut vom Blatt, und um alles in einem zu sagen: Er spielt größtentheils das wohltemperirte Clavier von Sebastian Bach, welches ihm Herr Neefe unter die Hände gegeben. Wer diese Sammlung von Präludien und Fugen durch alle Töne kennt, (welche man fast das non plus ultra nennen könnte,) wird wissen, was das bedeute. Herr Neefe hat ihm auch, sofern es seine übrige Geschäfte erlaubten, einige Anleitung zum Generalbaß gegeben. Jetzt übt er ihn in der Composition, und zu seiner Ermunterung hat er 9 Variationen von ihm fürs Clavier über einen Marsch in Mannheim stechen lassen. Dieses junge Genie verdiente Unterstützung, daß er reisen könnte. Er würde gewiß ein zweyter Wolfgang Amadeus Mozart werden, wenn er so fortschritte, wie er angefangen.

"THREE SONATAS FOR PIANO," DEDICATED TO
MAXIMILIAN FRIEDRICH, ARCHBISHOP AND KURFÜRST
OF COLOGNE

These works were written when the composer was eleven years old. They were published in 1783 by Bossler in Speyer. (Society of Friends of Music, Vienna)

Title page

Dedication

41

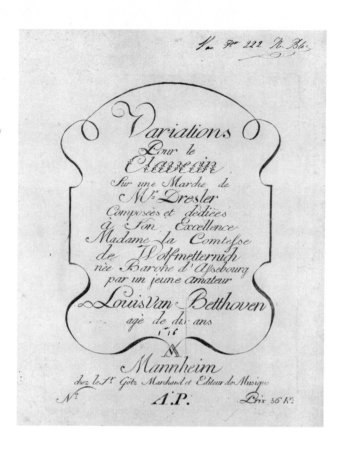

**"VARIATIONS POUR LE CLAVECIN
SUR UNE MARCHE DE DRESSLER"**

Front page with dedication to the Countess Wolff-Metternich

This work, written in 1782, is the first published piece of Beethoven. It was published by Götz in Mannheim in 1782. (Collection Aloys Mooser, University Library, Geneva)

"TO AN INFANT," LIED

The little piece written in 1783 was first published in the collection "Neue Blumenlese für Klavierliebhaber" by Bossler in Speyer in 1784. (Beethoven Archive, Bonn)

AUTOGRAPH OF "VARIATIONEN ÜBER EIN SCHWEIZER LIED"

Composed in Bonn in 1790, this work was printed in 1798 by N. Simrock, Bonn, under the title: "Six variations faciles d'un air Suisse pour la Harpe ou le Forte-Piano par L. van Beethoven." (Bodmer, Zürich)

8 Johan Beethoven

9 Ferdinandt Heller

14. Ludwig Beethoven

15. Johan Ries

MEMORANDA CONCERNING MUSIC AT THE COURT OF BONN (1784)

After the death of Kurfürst Maximilian Friedrich, his successor Maximilian Franz, an ardent admirer of music, requested a report on the state of the orchestra of his diocese. There is a detailed appraisal of each musician. On the left the report on Johann van Beethoven, on the right that on Ludwig. Because of this report the new ruler appointed Ludwig, despite his fourteen years, second organist subordinated to his teacher Neefe, and with an annual salary of 150 Gulden. (State Archive, Düsseldorf)

AUGUSTUSBURG PALACE AT BRÜHL, SUMMER RESIDENCE OF THE KURFÜRST OF COLOGNE
Engraving by Mettely after J. M. Metz

Whenever the Archbishop and his court went to Brühl, half way between Bonn and Cologne, all the musicians travelled with them. When the orchestra performed in the magnificent Baroque parlor of the Brühl palace, young Beethoven had the opportunity to play the harpsichord or the viola. (Municipal Archive, Bonn)

43

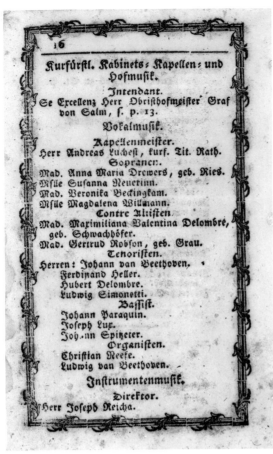

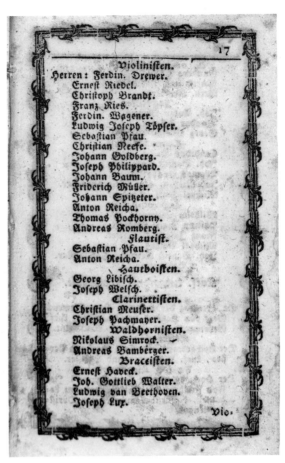

"COLOGNE COURT AND ADDRESS CALENDAR FOR THE YEAR 1792"

In the Calendar, which also lists personnel of the Archbishop's Court, we find (page 16) Johann van Beethoven as "first tenor," and on the same and the following pages his son Ludwig as second "organist" (together with his teacher Neefe) and as third "violist." Beethoven's friend Anton Reicha, who later became professor at the Paris Conservatory, is listed among the violinists and as second "flautist." (Municipal Archive, Bonn)

GERHARD FRIEDRICH W. GROSSMANN
(1746—1796)

Engraving by Geyser after Cöntgen

Grossmann was director of Seyler's actors troupe, which was called to the Bonn National Theater by Kurfürst Maximilian Friedrich. His daughter-in-law, Friedrike Flittner, was the star of the Bonn Opera for five years. (Beethovenhaus, Bonn)

FRANZ ANTON RIES (1755—1846)
Wax medallion

The distinguished first violinist of the electoral orchestra at Bonn not only was one of the teachers of the young Beethoven, but remained a lifelong friend and benefactor of the Beethoven family. (Collection Wegeler, Koblenz)

BERNHARD ROMBERG (1767—1841)

Lithograph by Gentili after Krüger

One of the most renowned cellists of his time.

ANDREAS ROMBERG (1767—1821)

After an unidentified engraving

Violist and composer. He also set Schiller's "Die Glocke" to music.

The cousins Bernhard and Andreas Romberg were members of the electoral orchestra at Bonn as was young Beethoven (1790—93). All three were to meet later in Vienna. (National Library Vienna; Beethovenhaus, Bonn)

NICOLAS SIMROCK (1752—1834)

After a lithograph by Weber

Simrock, archivist and horn player of the electoral orchestra at Bonn, always was a generous friend of the Beethoven family. In 1790 he founded the famous publishing house still bearing his name and published several of Beethoven's early works. (Beethovenhaus, Bonn)

ABBÉ FRANZ XAVER STERKEL (1750—1817)

After a lithograph by H. E. Wintter

This distinguished pianist and skillful composer undoubtedly influenced young Beethoven by his brilliant playing as well as by his pleasant compositions. (Beethovenhaus, Bonn)

LUDWIG VAN BEETHOVEN
AT THE AGE OF SIXTEEN (1786)
Silhouette by Neesen

The earliest known portrait of the young musician. Fischer describes him in his diary at that time: "short, squat, broad shoulders, short neck, big head, round nose, dark brown complexion, always walking slightly bent over. At home they called the boy 'der Spagnol' . . ."

COUNTESS ANNA HORTENSIA VON HATZFELDT
Oil painting

The Countess was a facile pianist, trained in singing and in playing the piano by the best Viennese teachers. Influential and enthusiastic, she sponsored musicians, and particularly young Beethoven. (Prince von Hatzfeldt, Trachenberg)

COUNTESS FÉLISE WOLFF-METTERNICH
Oil painting by Beckenkamp

One of the eminent personalities of the court at Bonn. She took an interest in Beethoven, who dedicated his «Variations pour le clavecin sur une Marche de Dressler» to her (see page 42). (Count Wolff-Metternich, Castle Gracht)

FRANZ GERHARD WEGELER (1765—1848)

Silhouette by Neesen

Though five years older than Ludwig van Beethoven, Wegeler became one of the best friends of the composer. Professor of medicine and Dean of Bonn University, he, in order to escape from the French Revolution in 1794, fled to Beethoven in Vienna. (Wegeler Archive, Koblenz)

CARL AUGUST BARON VON MALCHUS (1770—1840)

Oil painting by Schlaberg

Born in 1770, like Beethoven, Malchus belonged to the circle of intimate friends of the composer. In 1813 he became Secretary of the Interior of Jérôme Napoléon, King of Westphalia. (Private Collection, Wiesbaden)

ANTON REICHA (1770—1836)

Engraving by M. F. Dien after Cunis

Born in the same year as Beethoven, Reicha was his colleague as a flautist in the Archbishop's orchestra at Bonn and was a faithful friend to young Ludwig. They were to meet again in Vienna. (Conservatory of Music, Paris)

MARIA ANNA WILHELMINE BARONESS VON WESTERHOLT
Oil painting

Three years younger than Beethoven, she met him at the home of Frau von Breuning.
She became a pupil of the young master and one of his first and passionate romances.
Later she married Baron von Beverförde-Werries. (Baron von Beverförde-Werries,
Castle Loburg)

BEETHOVEN LETTER
TO BARONESS VON WESTERHOLT

This note to his friend very likely was written when he
had just fallen in love, apparently in 1790. (Beethovenhaus, Bonn)

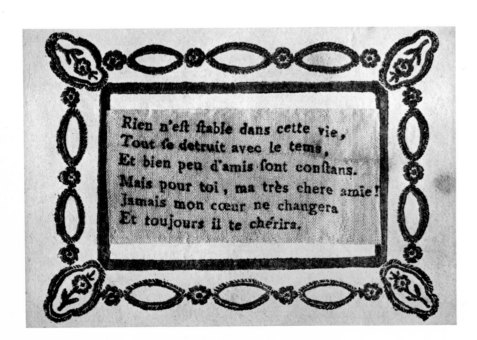

48

THE TWIN BROTHERS GERHARD (1772—1820)
AND CARL (1772—1832) VON KÜGELGEN
Oil portrait by G. v. Kügelgen

The two painter brothers, one a portraitist, the other a landscape
painter, became friends of Beethoven. They had made his acquaintance at the home of Frau von Breuning. It should be
remembered that the so-called Beethoven portrait by Kügelgen
is apocryphal in spite of the sensation it created when discovered
at the end of the 19th century. (Private Collection)

BABETTE KOCH,
WIFE OF COUNT BELDERBUSCH (1771—1807)
Oil painting

Babette Koch's mother owned the renowned restaurant "Der
Zehrgarten" at the market square of Bonn. Babette was an intimate friend of Eleonore von Breuning. She was married to
Count Anton von Belderbusch and died at the age of 36. (Baron
von Boeselager, Heimerzheim)

THE BONN MARKET SQUARE
Engraving by Hundeshagen

Center background is the Bonn Town Hall. At the right, on the other side of the street, was the restaurant "Der Zehrgarten," managed by Babette Koch's
mother. It was a meeting place not only of artists, but of society as well. Here young Beethoven frequently met a group of refined people. His friend Wegeler
later wrote that to Beethoven Babette Koch was a woman "nearest to perfection." (Municipal Archive, Bonn)

BEETHOVEN AND THE FAMILY OF "FRAU HOFRÄTIN VON BREUNING"

After his friend F. G. Wegeler had introduced him to the von Breuning family of Bonn, Beethoven soon became more than a good friend of the young Breunings—an adopted son of "Frau Hofrätin." Frau von Breuning gave the young musician the attention and care of which he had been deprived since his mother's death in 1787.

THE BREUNING HOUSE ON THE MÜNSTERPLATZ IN BONN
Drawing by M. Frickel

Beethoven was well received in this hospitable home, open to the friends of the Breunings at all times. He was treated so cordially that the young artist gratefully regarded Frau von Breuning as a second mother. (Municipal Archive, Bonn)

CHRISTOPH VON BREUNING (1771—1814)
Miniature by G. von Kügelgen
(Beethovenhaus, Bonn)

STEPHAN VON BREUNING (1774—1827)
Miniature by G. von Kügelgen
(Beethovenhaus, Bonn)

HELENE VON BREUNING, NÉE VON KERICH (1751—1838)
Miniature by G. von Kügelgen

Helene von Breuning, widow of the Councillor Emanuel Joseph von Breuning, killed in a fire of the Archbishop's palace in January, 1777, devoted herself entirely to the education of her four children Christoph, Eleonore, Stephan, and Lorenz. (Beethovenhaus, Bonn)

TEATIME WITH FRAU VON BREUNING
Silhouette by an unknown artist

Left to right: Canon von Kerich, brother of Helene von Breuning, and her daughter Eleonore. The latter, Beethoven's first love, was never quite forgotten. She later married his good friend Franz Gerhard Wegeler. No portrait of Eleonore exists other than these two silhouettes. (Wegeler Family, Koblenz)

FRAU VON BREUNING WITH HER CHILDREN AND THE CANON VON KERICH (1782)
Silhouette by an unknown artist

Both Eleonore von Breuning and her younger brother Lorenz were piano pupils of Beethoven. Christoph and Stephan studied law, Lorenz studied medicine. (Frau von Nell, Trier)

GREETING CARDS OF BEETHOVEN, TO ELEONORE VON BREUNING
One card is dated 1791. (Wegeler Family, Koblenz)

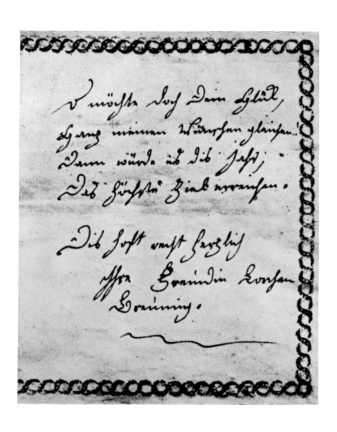

NEW YEAR'S GREETINGS OF ELEONORE VON BREUNING TO BEETHOVEN
Address and contents in Eleonore's hand. (Wegeler Family, Koblenz)

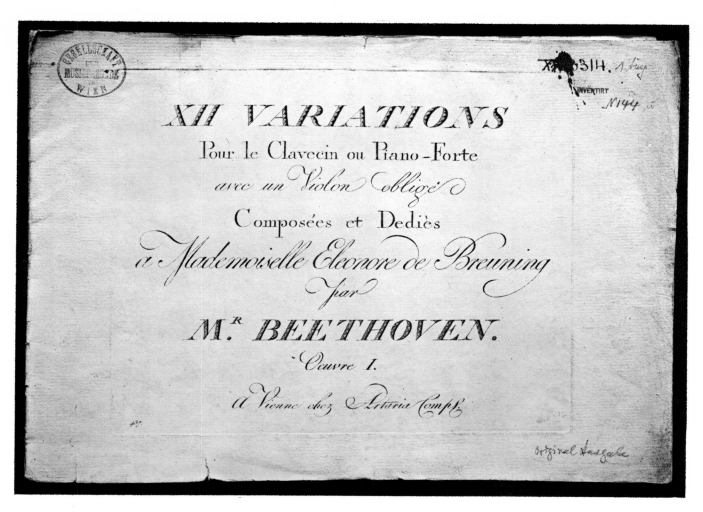

"XII VARIATIONS POUR LE CLAVECIN AVEC UN VIOLON OBLIGÉ"
Title page with dedication to Eleonore von Breuning

These variations were composed by Beethoven in 1792—93. They were published by Artaria in Vienna in July, 1793. The title page pictured is that of the edition of 1794. (Society of Friends of Music, Vienna)

FRANZ GERHARD WEGELER (1765—1848)
After a lithograph

Having completed his studies at Bonn University, and after an involuntary stay in Vienna, Wegeler settled in Koblenz as a physician. Later he married Eleonore von Breuning. He maintained most cordial relations with Beethoven. (Beethovenhaus, Bonn)

VASE OF BOHEMIAN CRYSTAL
GIVEN TO BEETHOVEN BY WEGELER

(Wegeler Family, Koblenz)

VIENNA, VIEW FROM THE JOSEFSTADT (1785)
Colored engraving by Carl Schütz

The time of Beethoven's departure for Vienna and of his stay there is not exactly known. His trip took place in the spring of 1787. He entered the Imperial city for the first time on April 7th. Most probably the Archbishop of Cologne introduced him to his brother, Emperor Joseph II, and to Mozart. Beethoven would have liked to study under Haydn and Mozart, at least for a period. (Historical Museum of the City of Vienna)

WOLFGANG AMADEUS MOZART (1756—1791)
Engraving by Giovanni Bosio after Sasso

It is uncertain whether Mozart gave young Beethoven lessons, but when Beethoven ingeniously improvised on the piano in his presence, Mozart is quoted as having said: "Watch him, he will make the world remember him." (Mozart Museum, Salzburg)

EMPEROR JOSEPH II (1741—1790)
Engraving by Friedrich John after Heinrich Friedrich Füger

It is not certain whether Beethoven was presented to the Emperor. Perhaps he attended a soirée at court as one of the many guests. When he left Vienna, however, both the Emperor and Mozart had impressed him deeply. (National Library, Vienna)

Beethoven, informed by his family that his mother was seriously ill, immediately left Vienna and hurried back to Bonn. Although he travelled at great speed he arrived home but shortly before his mother's death. Her passing touched him deeply.

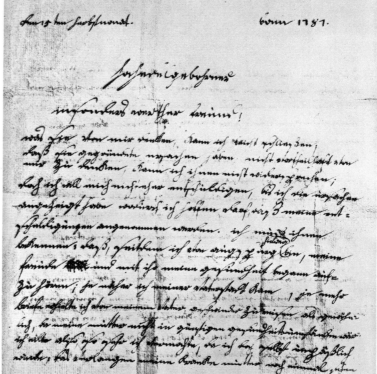

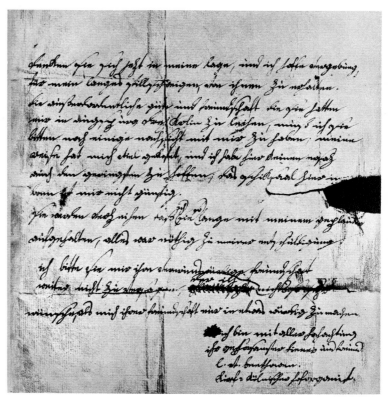

LETTER OF BEETHOVEN TO THE COUNCILLOR VON SCHADEN IN AUGSBURG (Autumn, 1787)

The oldest Beethoven letter preserved. Most important is the part concerning his mother's death and the decisive consequences resulting therefrom. (Beethovenhaus, Bonn)

COUNT FERDINAND ERNST VON WALDSTEIN (1762—1823)

Silhouette from Beethoven's album

The Count was an Austrian. When his friend, Archduke Maximilian Franz, was appointed Kurfürst of Cologne, the Count followed him to Bonn. Waldstein, himself a gifted musician and composer, made Beethoven's acquaintance in Frau von Breuning's home and immediately became interested in him. He probably helped promote Beethoven's appointment as court organist. Later he frequently helped his young protégé and finally convinced the Kurfürst of the necessity of sending Beethoven to Vienna so he would be able to complete his education. (National Library, Vienna)

PAGE OF BEETHOVEN'S MANUSCRIPT OF THE PIANO VERSION OF THE "RITTERBALLET"

Beethoven composed the "Ritterballet" in 1790—91. On March 6, 1791, the nobility performed it on the occasion of Mardi gras at the Bonn Palace. Composition and choreography are ascribed to Waldstein! The Former State Library (Berlin) is in possession of the orchestral score of this composition. The piano version was published in 1872, the orchestral score in 1888. (Beethovenhaus, Bonn)

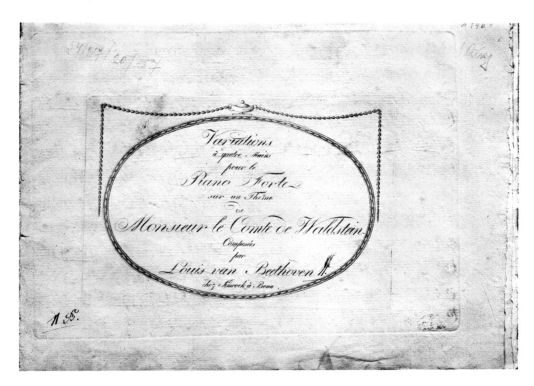

"VARIATIONS À QUATRE MAINS POUR LE PIANO-FORTE"
Title page with dedication to Count von Waldstein

Variations on a theme composed by the Count. They were written during Beethoven's last Bonn period, 1791—92. The first edition was published by Simrock, Bonn, in 1794. The manuscript is in the library of the Paris Conservatory. (Society of Friends of Music, Vienna)

AUTOGRAPH OF THE RONDO FOR EIGHT WIND INSTRUMENTS IN E FLAT

The work was composed in 1792 for two oboes, two clarinets, two bassoons, and two horns, as dinner music for the court of the Kurfürst Maximilian Franz. It was published in 1830, after Beethoven's death, by Diabelli in Vienna, under the title "Rondino für achtstimmige Harmonie" (Rondino for eight part harmony). (Beethovenhaus, Bonn)

"BEETHOVEN'S ALBUM"

Before leaving for Vienna Beethoven invited all his friends to the restaurant "Zehrgarten," owned by the mother of Babette Koch. His friends donated the then customary album to him. Each had contributed a dedication, a few verses, or a drawing to it. The page shown above bears the signature of Babette Koch's brother. (National Library, Vienna)

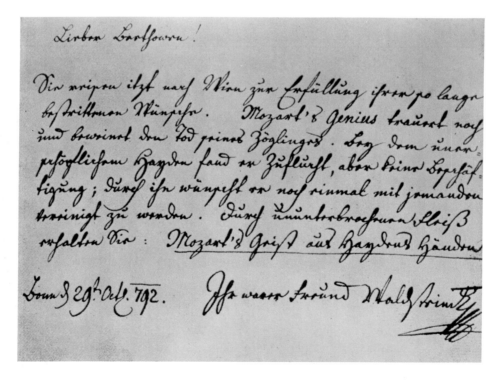

COUNT VON WALDSTEIN'S CONTRIBUTION TO THE BEETHOVEN ALBUM

(National Library, Vienna)

BEETHOVEN'S FIRST VIENNESE PERIOD (November, 1792)

Owing to Count von Waldstein's efforts the young composer was given the Kurfürst's permission to complete his studies under Haydn in Vienna. Soon after arriving there, he received the news of his father's passing (December 18). In spite of a modest stipend from the Kurfürst, Beethoven's first Viennese period was characterized by his financial state, which often was depressing.

VIENNA AS SEEN FROM BELVEDERE
Oil painting by B. Bellotto, called "Il Canaletto"

Beyond the park of the palace one can see the Schwarzenberg castle and the Imperial stables. In the background, center, St. Stephan's Tower. The splendid architecture of the Imperial city impressed Beethoven deeply. (National Gallery, Vienna)

"DER GRABEN" TOWARDS "KOHLMARKT"
Colored engraving by C. Schütz

In about 1800 Beethoven lived at "214 Auf dem Graben," on the third floor. The first house on the right, one of five floors, was that of the printer and bookseller Trattner. In the background at the right was "Die Jungferngasse," leading to the "Petersplatz." On "Paternostergässchen," at the left, the shop of the music publisher Haslinger, one of Beethoven's friends, was located. (Historical Museum of the City of Vienna)

59

"MICHAELERPLATZ," VIENNA
Colored engraving by C. Schütz

Left: St. Michael's Church. On the other side, under the dome, the famous riding school frequently used for concerts. At the extreme right, the charming Imperial-Royal Court Theater where many of Beethoven's works were produced as soon as they were completed. (Historical Museum of the City of Vienna)

"SCHOTTENKIRCHE" AND "BIS AUF DEM HOF" (a square)
Colored engraving by C. Schütz

The two most attractive buildings of this square were Count Kinsky's and Count Harrasch's palaces. At the right, Count Kinsky's palace, where a carriage is stopping. In the center, a lane leads to the square "Am Hofe." At the left the "Tiefer Graben," where Beethoven lived at the end of the year 1800, terminates. (Historical Museum of the City of Vienna)

JOSEPH HAYDN (1732—1809)

Engraving by Johann Ernst Mansfeld

Beethoven had obtained permission to go to Vienna in order to become a pupil of Haydn. He immediately began his study under the great master—the greatest since Mozart's death—and remained his student until 1794, the time of Haydn's trip to London. (Mozart Museum, Salzburg)

"TROIS SONATES POUR LE CLAVECIN," OPUS 2

Title page with dedication to Haydn

The three sonatas, which were published by Artaria in Vienna in 1796, are dedicated to his great teacher, in gratitude. (van Hoboken, Ascona)

JOHANN GEORG ALBRECHTSBERGER (1736—1809)
Oil painting

The court organist and director of the orchestra at St. Stephan, Albrechtsberger was also a distinguished composer and theorist. He became Beethoven's counterpoint teacher when Haydn went to London in 1794, and taught him until May, 1795. (Society of Friends of Music, Vienna)

ANTON SALIERI (1750—1825)
Oil painting

Salieri, director of the court orchestra and a skillful composer, had been a resident of Vienna since 1766. From 1793 to 1802 Beethoven studied stage music composition with him and later occasionally asked his advice. (Society of Friends of Music, Vienna)

JOHANN SCHENK (1754—1836)
Oil painting

Beethoven tried to broaden his knowledge of theory by studying with Schenk, a very popular operatic composer in Vienna. Both he and Schenk kept the teacher-pupil relationship confidential. (Society of Friends of Music, Vienna)

EMANUEL ALOIS FÖRSTER (1748—1823)
Lithograph by Joseph Teltscher

Förster, an esteemed composer and a fine teacher, particularly of counterpoint, received Beethoven with great friendliness and gave him good advice, which later proved beneficial to his composition of quartets. (Historical Museum of the City of Vienna)

"Exercise in counterpoint for two parts with syncopation"

Page from a Beethoven study book

Notice the remarks by Beethoven's hand: "If a measure with no ties occurs it may be filled with un-tied half-beats."—At the end of the page: "Fifth species of counterpoint. Contrapunctum floridum, the ornamented counterpoint, since even at that time embellishment, flowing movements, and other varieties of the species occurred." In the fourth example he called the third measure "bad" with reference to open fifths lagging behind. (Society of Friends of Music, Vienna)

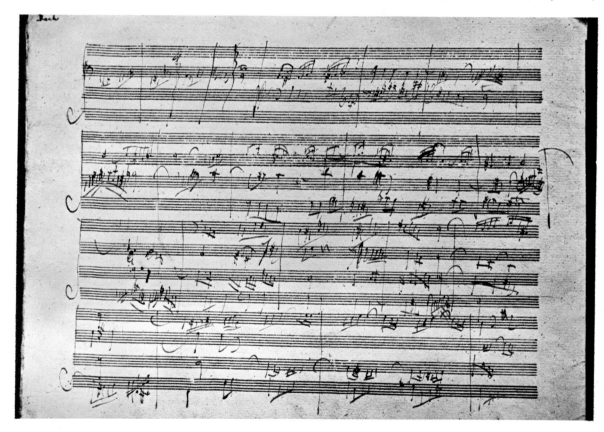

Copy of the Fugue in B minor from Johann Sebastian Bach's
"Well tempered keyboard" arranged for string quartet

Autograph by Ludwig van Beethoven

Undoubtedly an exercise from Beethoven's study period. (Society of Friends of Music, Vienna)

PROGRAM OF THE MUSICAL
ACADEMY AT THE BURGTHEATER,
MARCH 29, 1795

In this concert Beethoven performed his Second Piano Concerto, opus 19, which he had just completed, but which was still unpublished. The evening had been arranged for the benefit of the "Widows' and Orphans' Fund of the Society of Musicians." (National Library, Vienna)

THE NATIONAL COURT THEATER
OF VIENNA

Colored engraving by Tranquillo Mollo

The concert mentioned above took place in this theater. The following day Beethoven participated in another concert in which he played brilliant piano improvisations. On March 31st he played a Mozart piano concerto in a concert arranged by Mozart's widow ... In the same hall the ballet music to "Die Geschöpfe des Prometheus" was performed in 1801, and in 1810, the music to "Egmont" was heard. (Historical Museum of the City of Vienna)

FIRST PIANO CONCERTO, C MAJOR, OPUS 15, BY LUDWIG VAN BEETHOVEN

Title page with dedication to his pupil Princess Odescalchi, née Countess Keglevics

This concerto, composed in 1795—96 and then again in 1798, was completed only after the Concerto for Piano and Orchestra, No. 2, B flat major, opus 19. Probably it was first performed by Beethoven himself in Prague in 1798. It was published by T. Mollo in Vienna in 1801, after the Countess' marriage to Prince Odescalchi. (van Hoboken, Ascona)

REVIEW OF THE CONCERT
OF MARCH 29, 1795

An excerpt from the *Wiener Staats-zeitung* of April 1, 1795. (Municipal Library, Vienna)

"DER KOHLMARKT" IN VIENNA
Colored engraving by L. Beyer

One of the main streets of Vienna on which Artaria & Co. was located, the art and publishing house which published many of Beethoven's works. The Artaria shop is in the foreground at the right. (Historical Museum of the City of Vienna)

CARLO ARTARIA (1747—1808)

Oil painting by Joseph Kreutzinger

In 1770 he founded, together with his cousin Francesco Artaria, the famous publishing house Artaria & Co. When arriving in Vienna Beethoven established contact with this firm. As early as 1793 his Variations for Violin and Piano on "Se vuol ballare" from Mozart's "Figaro," were published by Artaria. His contact with Artaria was lasting and friendly. (Archive Artaria, Vienna)

DOMENICO ARTARIA (1775—1842)

Oil painting by Peter Krafft

Domenico, Francesco Artaria's son, was the head of the firm after 1804. He continued the contact with Beethoven. (Archive Artaria, Vienna)

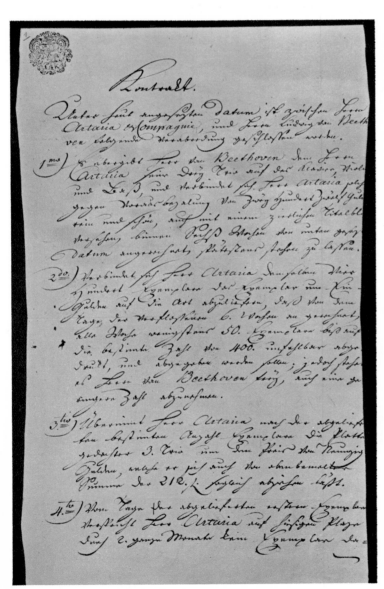

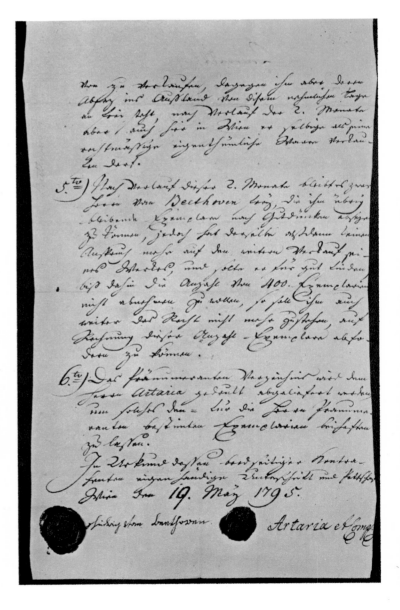

CONTRACT BETWEEN BEETHOVEN AND THE PUBLISHER C. ARTARIA (May 19, 1795)

In this contract Artaria assumes the printing of the Three Trios, opus 1, at the price of 212 florins; he also agrees to sell Beethoven 400 copies at 400 gulden. Beethoven retained the sale in Vienna for the first two months, at a price of one ducat per copy. After that Artaria was to continue the sale for its own account. Beethoven succeeded in having 241 copies of this Trios subscribed to. (Bodmer, Zürich)

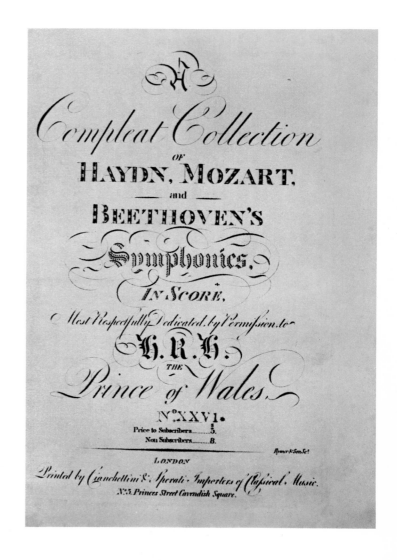

BARON GOTTFRIED VAN SWIETEN (1734—1803)

Engraving by J. Axmann after P. Fendi

Van Swieten, a diplomat, and later on director of the court library, was an ardent admirer of music. He had founded an association of lovers of classical music for the benefit of the aristocracy of Vienna; special attention was given to the music of Johann Sebastian Bach. He was one of the first to recognize and further Beethoven's talent. He introduced him to aristocratic circles and gave him the opportunity to become familiar with the works of Bach and Händel. (Society of Friends of Music, Vienna)

SYMPHONY No. 1, C MAJOR, OPUS 21

Orchestral parts

Title page of the first edition (left), published in 1801 by Hoffmeister & Cie, Vienna.

Score

Title page of the first edition (right), published in 1809 by Cianchettini & Sperati in London.

The First Symphony was composed 1799—1800 and dedicated to Beethoven's patron Baron van Swieten. The composer himself conducted the first performance on April 2, 1800. (Former State Library, Berlin; Library, British Museum, London)

PRINCESS MARIE CHRISTINE LICHNOWSKY
(1765—1841)
Engraving by C. Pfeiffer after J. Grassi
(National Library, Vienna)

PRINCE KARL LICHNOWSKY (1756—1814)
Oil painting
(Collection Prince Lichnowsky, Grätz)

Both not only supported Beethoven most generously, but also proved his true friends. Their rich home was always open to the genius who, nevertheless, occasionally was most annoying. They offered him, in addition to a room and a place at their table, a personal servant and instruments for an excellent string quartet (page 226). They ignored the frequent unpolished habits of their guest. The Princess made some futile attempts, however, to teach Beethoven, whom she treated like an adopted son, the "bon ton." At the Lichnowsky palace many of Beethoven's works received first performances.

TWELVE VARIATIONS FOR PIANO AND CELLO ON A THEME FROM HÄNDEL'S ORATORIO "JUDAS MACCABÄUS"
First page of the autograph

Composed in 1796 and published the following year by Artaria. The variations are dedicated to Princess Lichnowsky. (Society of Friends of Music, Vienna)

THREE TRIOS FOR PIANO, VIOLIN AND CELLO, OPUS 1

Title page with dedication to Prince Karl Lichnowsky; composed in 1793 and 1794. Published by Artaria in 1795.

When Haydn heard these trios at a soirée in the Lichnowsky palace he recommended to Beethoven that he destroy the C minor Trio as he considered it unworthy of the composer's talent. Beethoven, however, correctly believing this work to be the best of the three, began to suspect Haydn of jealousy. (Society of Friends of Music, Vienna)

SYMPHONY NO. 2, D MAJOR, OPUS 36

Title page with dedication to Prince Lichnowsky

Composed in 1802 and published by the Bureau d'Arts et d'Industrie in Vienna in 1804. The first edition of the score was published in 1808 by Cianchettini & Sperati in London. (van Hoboken, Ascona)

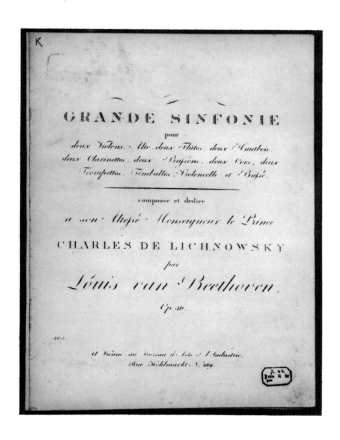

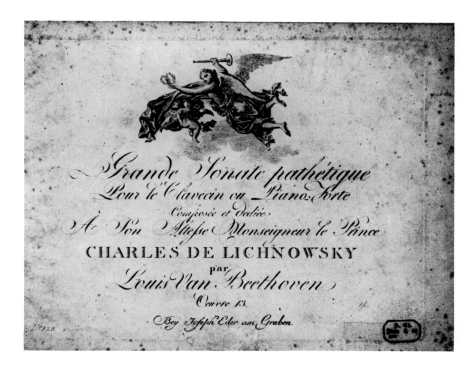

GRAND SONATA FOR PIANO, C MINOR, OPUS 13 (PATHÉTIQUE)

Title page with dedication to Prince Lichnowsky

The sonata was composed in 1798—99 and published by Joseph Eder in Vienna in 1799. (van Hoboken, Ascona)

GRAND SONATA FOR PIANO, IN A FLAT MAJOR, OPUS 26

Title page with dedication to Prince Lichnowsky

Composed in 1800—01 and published by J. Cappi in Vienna in 1802. (van Hoboken, Ascona)

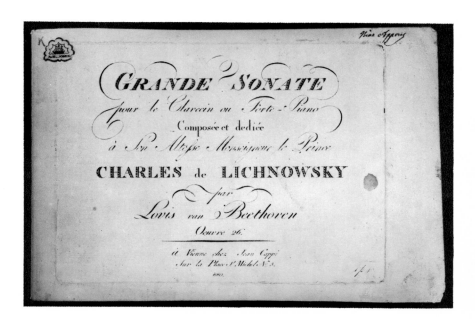

THE SCHUPPANZIGH QUARTET

The famous quartet founded by the eminent violinist Schuppanzigh above all had played chamber music by Haydn and Mozart before entering the services of Prince Lichnowsky. Then the quartet was at Beethoven's disposal and performed his works as soon as they were completed. Later the quartet was in the employ of Count Rasumoffsky, another Beethoven patron.

IGNAZ SCHUPPANZIGH (1776—1830)
Lithograph by B. Schrötter

Schuppanzigh, an excellent violinist and incomparable musician, and his ensemble were the ideal interpreters of Beethoven's music. He also established a record as a conductor. (Society of Friends of Music, Vienna)

JOSEPH MAYSEDER (1789—1863)
Engraving by Blasius Höfel after L. Létronne

Mayseder, a virtuoso and a capable composer, joined the quartet as a youth. Occasionally Prince Lichnowsky took his place as the second violinist. (Society of Friends of Music, Vienna)

NICOLAS KRAFT (1778—1855)
Pencil drawing by J. Alberti

This outstanding cellist was a member of the Schuppanzigh Quartet, as was the cellist Linke. (Society of Friends of Music, Vienna)

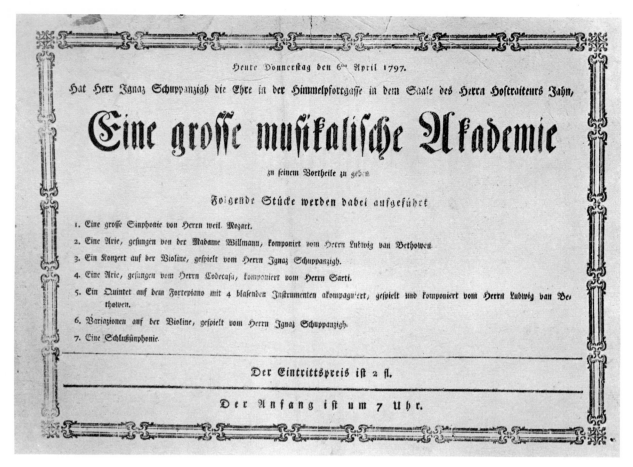

Heute Donnerstag den 6ᵗᵉⁿ April 1797.

Hat Herr Ignaz Schuppanzigh die Ehre in der Himmelpfortgasse in dem Saale des Herrn Hostraiteurs Jahn,

Eine grosse musikalische Akademie

zu seinem Vortheile zu geben

Folgende Stücke werden dabei aufgeführt

1. Eine grosse Sinphonie von Herrn weil. Mozart.
2. Eine Arie, gesungen von der Madame Willmann, komponiert vom Herrn Ludwig van Bethoven.
3. Ein Konzert auf der Violine, gespielt vom Herrn Ignaz Schuppanzigh.
4. Eine Arie, gesungen vom Herrn Codecasa, komponiert vom Herrn Sarti.
5. Ein Quintet auf dem Fortepiano mit 4 blasenden Instrumenten akompagniert, gespielt und komponiert vom Herrn Ludwig van Bethoven.
6. Variazionen auf der Violine, gespielt vom Herrn Ignaz Schuppanzigh.
7. Eine Schlußsinphonie.

Der Eintrittspreis ist 2 fl.

Der Anfang ist um 7 Uhr.

PROGRAM OF A MUSICAL ACADEMY GIVEN BY SCHUPPANZIGH AT THE JAHN
AUDITORIUM, APRIL 6, 1797

In this concert the audience of Vienna heard the Quintet for Piano and Wind Instruments, E flat major, opus 16, for the first time. Beethoven had dedicated the work to Prince Schwarzenberg and played the piano part himself (page 78). (Society of Friends of Music, Vienna)

THE CONCERT HALL AT THE AUGARTEN IN VIENNA
Colored engraving by L. Poratzky

In this hall in which Mozart had already appeared, the Schuppanzigh Quartet performed the "Morning Concerts," during which several Beethoven quartets were heard. Beethoven himself also appeared here, and together with the violinist Bridgetower played his "Kreutzer Sonata," opus 47, in May, 1803. Here he also conducted his Concerto for Piano, Violin, Cello and Orchestra, opus 56, in May, 1808. (Historical Museum of the City of Vienna)

Beethoven left Vienna in February, 1796, probably in the company of Prince Lichnowsky, and did not return until the beginning of the following summer.

THE NATIONAL THEATER OF PRAGUE
Water color by Vincenz Morstadt

In 1787 Mozart conducted a performance of "The Marriage of Figaro" and the première of "Don Giovanni" in this beautiful building, a gift of Count Nostitz. Beethoven spent several weeks in Prague playing not only his own compositions in his concerts, but also improvisations which won the favor of his audiences. His mastery of extemporization was incomparable. Upon departing from Prague he had made many friends plus a considerable amount of money. (City Museum, Prague)

THE SINGAKADEMIE IN BERLIN
Lithograph by Finden after Klose

Beethoven used the opportunity of his presence in the Prussian capital to play for the court and for larger audiences several times, primarily in the concert hall of the Singakademie. His skillful improvisations at the piano on themes given him by the audience apparently left a deeper impression than did his own compositions. (Former State Library, Berlin)

FREDERICK WILLIAM II, KING OF PRUSSIA (1744—1797)

Engraving by Sintzenich after Schröder

The nephew and successor of Frederick the Great, himself a music lover to whom masters such as Mozart and Boccherini had dedicated some of their works, received Beethoven, then 26 years old, with great cordiality. He had Beethoven play for him on several occasions, and on his departure presented him with a golden box filled with louis d'ors. (Former State Library, Berlin)

JEAN-LOUIS DUPORT (1741—1818)

Engraving by Madame Lingée after Charles-Nicolas Cochin

Beethoven, together with this excellent cellist, had played for the royal family in Berlin. (National Library, Vienna)

TWO GRAND SONATAS FOR PIANO AND VIOLONCELLO, OPUS 5

In gratitude Beethoven dedicated these sonatas to the King of Prussia. Together with Jean-Louis Duport, solo cellist at the court, he had performed them for the monarch. These sonatas were published by Artaria in Vienna in 1797. (van Hoboken, Ascona)

FRIEDRICH HEINRICH HIMMEL (1765—1814)

After an engraving, not signed

Himmel, a talented composer and conductor, met Beethoven in Berlin. Their friendship lasted but a short time. (Former State Library, Berlin)

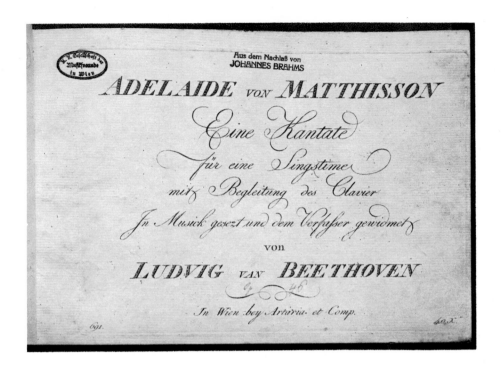

"ADELAIDE," CANTATA FOR ONE VOICE WITH PIANO, OPUS 46
Title page with dedication to the poet Friedrich Matthisson

Beethoven composed this cantata on a poem by Matthisson in 1796. It found the great acclaim of the public, which responded with greater enthusiasm to this work than it did to others of higher quality. First edition by Artaria in Vienna in 1797. (Society of Friends of Music, Vienna)

FRIEDRICH VON MATTHISSON
Engraving by W. Arndt after Tischbein

Beethoven was strongly influenced by the works of this famous poet. He composed several of his lyrics. (National Library, Vienna)

JOHANN WENZEL STICH, CALLED GIOVANNI PUNTO
(1748—1803)

Engraving by S.-C. Miger after Charles-Nicolas Cochin

Punto, a composer above all noted as a horn player of renown settled in Vienna in 1799. He established contact with Beethoven and taught him the technique of his instrument. Beethoven within 48 hours composed the Sonata for Horn and Piano, opus 17, which he played together with Punto at a benefit for invalids of the war. (National Library, Vienna)

SONATA FOR PIANO AND HORN, F MAJOR, OPUS 17
Title page with dedication to Baroness von Braun

Composed for Punto in April, 1800, published by T. Mollo in Vienna in 1801, and also by the Comptoir d'Industrie in Leipzig, and at Gayl & Hedler in Frankfurt. (van Hoboken, Ascona)

It is remarkable how many members of high society recognized Beethoven's genious and furthered his career. They did not seem disturbed by his urge for independence or his lack of manners.

COUNT MORITZ LICHNOWSKY (1771—1837)
Oil painting

He was a younger brother of Prince Karl, and as Karl an ardent musician. A former pupil of Mozart, he was a more gifted pianist than his older brother. All his life he was a sincere friend to Beethoven. On several occasions his influence prevented the undisciplined musician from suffering serious difficulties. (Collection Lichnowsky, Grätz)

FIFTEEN PIANO VARIATIONS WITH FUGUE, E FLAT MAJOR, OPUS 35
Title page with dedication to Count Moritz Lichnowsky

These variations are written on a theme from "The Creatures of Prometheus." They were composed in 1802 and published by Breitkopf & Härtel in Leipzig in 1803. (Society of Friends of Music, Vienna)

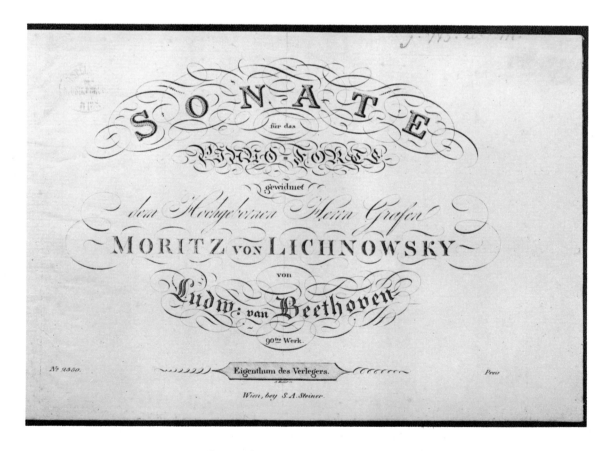

PIANO SONATA, E MINOR, OPUS 90
Title page with dedication to Count Moritz Lichnowsky

Composed in 1814, published by S. A. Steiner in Vienna in 1815. (Society of Friends of Music, Vienna)

JOSEPHINE, PRINCESS VON LIECHTENSTEIN,
NÉE PRINCESS VON FÜRSTENBERG
(1776—1836)
After an engraving, not signed
The Princess studied piano playing under Beethoven's
guidance. In appreciation of her talent the composer dedicated his "Sonata quasi una Fantasia per il Clavicembalo,"
opus 27, No. 1, to her. (National Library, Vienna)

JOHANN JOSEPH, PRINCE VON LIECHTENSTEIN
(1768—1836)
Engraving by Pichler after Friedrich Heinrich Füger

The prince maintained an orchestra and sponsored concerts in
his palace. (National Library, Vienna)

"SONATA QUASI UNA FANTASIA PER IL CLAVICEMBALO" IN E FLAT MAJOR, OPUS 27, No. 1
Title page with dedication to Princess von Liechtenstein

The sonata was composed ca. 1801 and was published as the first of two piano sonatas, opus 27, Nos. 1 and 2, by Cappi in Vienna
in March, 1802. (Society of Friends of Music, Vienna)

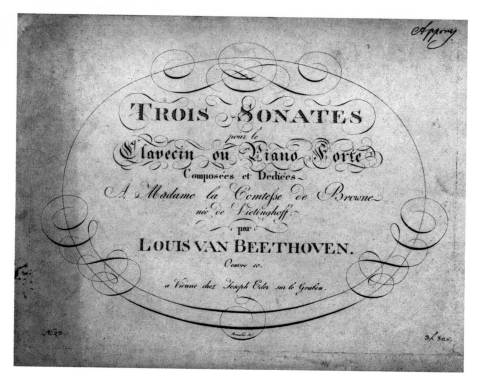

JOHANN GEORG IMPERIAL COUNT
VON BROWNE-CAMUS (1767—1827)
Engraving by J. G. Mansfeld

THREE PIANO SONATAS, OPUS 10
Title page with dedication to Countess von Browne

These sonatas were published by Joseph Eder in Vienna in July, 1798 and offered by subscription. (van Hoboken, Ascona)

Beethoven from 1798 to 1804 had a fervent and generous patron in the Count von Browne, «le premier mécène de ma muse», as he wrote somewhat unfairly in view of Prince Lichnowsky's equal generosity. Beethoven dedicated a number of his works to Count von Browne, particularly Seven Variations for piano and cello on a theme from Mozart's "Magic Flute"; Three Trios for violin, viola and cello, opus 9; the Piano Sonata, opus 22; and Six Lieder for piano and voice on poems by Gellert, opus 48. To the Count's wife, Anna Margerita Browne, née Vietinghoff, Beethoven dedicated the three sonatas for piano, opus 10; 12 Variations for piano "on a Russian Theme," and 6 Variations for piano "on a Theme by Süssmayr."

GRAND SONATA FOR PIANO, B FLAT MAJOR, OPUS 22
Title page with dedication to Count von Browne

The work, composed in 1800, was published by Hoffmeister in Vienna in 1802. (van Hoboken, Ascona)

QUINTET FOR PIANO, OBOE, CLARINET, BASSOON AND HORN,
E FLAT MAJOR, OPUS 16

Title page with dedication to Prince Schwarzenberg

At an "Academy" arranged by Schuppanzigh Beethoven played the piano part
of this quintet when it was premiered on April 6, 1797. The performance was
a great success. The work was published by T. Mollo in Vienna in 1801. (van
Hoboken, Ascona)

JOSEPH JOHANN, PRINCE VON SCHWARZENBERG
(1769—1833)

Engraving by C. Pfeiffer after J. Oelenhainz

Prince Schwarzenberg also maintained a house orchestra. In his
palace the Septet, opus 20, was first performed. Beethoven dedicated
his Quintet, opus 16, to him. (National Library, Vienna)

COUNT AND COUNTESS MORITZ VON FRIES
WITH THEIR SON

Oil painting by Baron von Gérard

Count von Fries, a passionate music lover, arranged some
of the finest concerts in his palace. A spendthrift, he also
was one of Beethoven's most generous patrons. Beethoven
dedicated some of his most important works to him: the
Sonatas for piano and violin, opus 23 and 24, the String
Quintet, opus 29, and the Seventh Symphony, opus 92.
(National Library, Vienna)

QUINTET FOR TWO VIOLINS, TWO VIOLAS,
AND VIOLONCELLO, C MAJOR, OPUS 29

Title page with dedication to Count von Fries

The quintet was completed in 1801. Since Artaria had failed
him, Beethoven had it published by Breitkopf & Härtel in
Leipzig in 1802. Irritated by such procedure, Artaria immediately printed a second edition, claiming that it was "a
revised and corrected version by Beethoven himself." (van
Hoboken, Ascona)

SONATA FOR PIANO AND VIOLIN, F MAJOR, OPUS 24
Title page with dedication to Count von Fries

This so-called "Spring Sonata" was published by T. Mollo in Vienna in 1801. The errors contained in the title of the first edition are explained by the fact that originally the two sonatas opus 23 and opus 24 were to be published as one single opus. (van Hoboken, Ascona)

MANUSCRIPT OF THE "SPRING SONATA," OPUS 24
First page of the manuscript

At the beginning of the work the author wrote "Sonata da L. v. Beethoven," further down on the same page his note to the copyist: "All abbreviations are to be written in full." (National Library, Vienna)

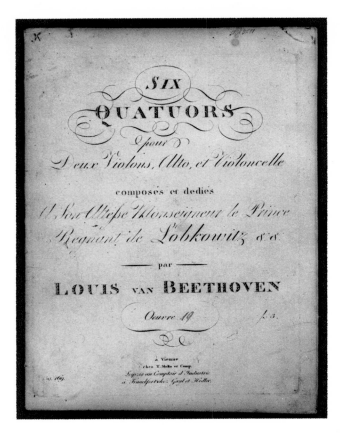

SIX QUARTETS FOR TWO VIOLINS, VIOLA AND
VIOLONCELLO, OPUS 18 AND 19

The first three quartets were published as opus 18 by Mollo in
Vienna in June, 1801, the other three as opus 19 in October of
the same year. Later the six quartets were joined and called
opus 18. (van Hoboken, Ascona)

PRINCE LOBKOWITZ' PALACE IN VIENNA
After a water color by R. Reuss
(Historical Museum of the City of Vienna)

FRANZ JOSEPH MAX, PRINCE LOBKOWITZ (1772—1816)
Engraving by C. Pfeiffer after J. Oelenhainz

The Prince, himself a violinist, met Beethoven soon after his arrival in Vienna.
Enchanted by the young genius, he patronized Beethoven and was a constant
friend until his death. Beethoven showed his gratitude by dedicating to him
the Six Quartets, opus 18 (1801), the Concerto for piano, violin and cello, opus
56 (1807), the Quartet, opus 74 (1810), the song cycle "To the Immortal
Beloved," opus 98 (1816), and above all the "Eroica," opus 55 (1806).
To both the Prince and Count Rasumoffsky he also dedicated the Fifth Symphony, opus 67, and the "Pastoral Symphony," opus 68 (1809). Many of Beethoven's works were performed by the orchestra of the Lobkowitz palace.
(National Library, Vienna)

THE BRUNSWICK FAMILY

"Our deep and sincere friendship with Beethoven lasted until his death. He came to Ofen, he came to Martonvásár, he was accepted into our circle of highly select people. A circle was built and planted with high and noble linden trees each bearing the name of one member; even when they were absent and we missed them, we talked to their symbols and conversed with and informed ourselves through them. Often, after bidding the tree "good morning," I asked all sorts of things; and whatever I wished to know, it never refused me the answer." (From the Memoirs of Therese von Brunswick)

THERESE COUNTESS VON BRUNSWICK (1775—1861)
Oil painting by J. B. de Lampi, the older

The Countess was a very gifted pupil of Beethoven, who fell passionately in love with her. She, too, showed such great affection for him that it was suggested that the famous letter "To the Immortal Beloved" found after Beethoven's death might have been addressed to her. It is certain, however, that Beethoven dedicated the piano sonata, opus 78 to her and that he carefully kept her portrait, reproduced above. (Beethovenhaus, Bonn)

INSCRIPTION ON THE BACK OF THE PORTRAIT OF THERESE VON BRUNSWICK
The inscription might have been written by Therese herself

DEM SELTNEN GENIE
DEM GROSSEN KÜNSTLER
DEM GUTEN MENSHEN
VON   T·B:

JOSEPHINE COUNTESS DEYM, LATER BARONESS STACKELBERG, NÉE BRUNSWICK (1779—1821)
Ivory miniature

Was she, the sister of Franz and Therese von Brunswick, perhaps the one addressed in that letter "To the Immortal Beloved"? It is certain that Beethoven was passionately in love with her, as thirteen letters addressed to her prove. These remained unknown until published in 1957. However the Countess probably did not reciprocate Beethoven's love. (Bodmer, Zürich)

FRANZ COUNT VON BRUNSWICK (1777—1849)
Oil painting by Tugut

He was his sister Therese's junior by two years. His ties to Beethoven were so close that in addressing one another they used the familiar *du* despite the difference in social position. During a stay at Martonvásár (1806) Beethoven composed the "Appassionata" for his friend and dedicated the Fantasy for piano, opus 77 (1810) to him. (Former Collection Figdor, Vienna)

LIED WITH VARIATIONS FOR PIANO, FOUR HANDS, ON THE POEM "ICH DENKE DEIN"

This was Beethoven's first composition on Goethe lyrics. Beethoven wrote four of the variations in the album of Josephine and Therese von Brunswick in May, 1799. He added two more before they were published by the Comptoir d'Art et d'Industrie in Vienna in 1805. (Society of Friends of Music, Vienna)

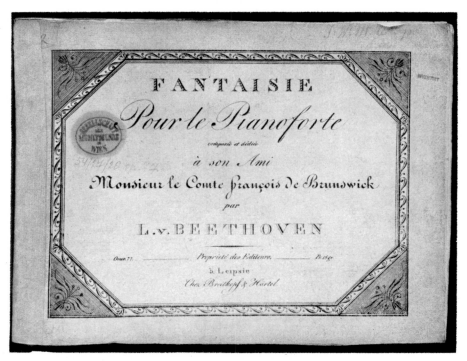

FANTASY FOR PIANO, G MINOR, OPUS 77
Title page with dedication to Count Franz von Brunswick

The Fantasy was composed in October 1809 and published by Breitkopf & Härtel in 1810. (Society of Friends of Music, Vienna)

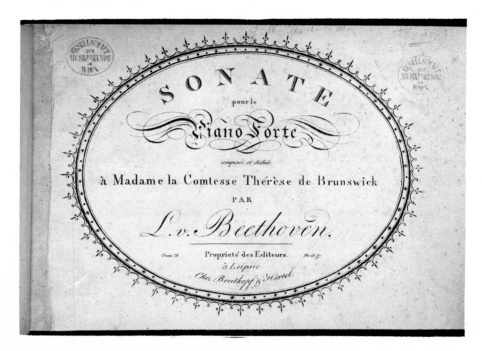

PIANO SONATA, F SHARP MAJOR, OPUS 78
Title page
with dedication to Countess Therese von Brunswick

This Sonata, created in 1809 and published simultaneously by Breitkopf & Härtel and Artaria in 1810, is the only work Beethoven dedicated to his friend Therese. Why he failed to dedicate any of his more important works to her is hard to understand. (Society of Friends of Music, Vienna)

PIANO SONATA, F MINOR, OPUS 57, SO-CALLED "APPASSIONATA"
Title page with dedication to Count Franz von Brunswick

According to Ries Beethoven created this grandiose work in Döbling in 1804. Schindler, however, believes that he wrote it in 1806, all at once, while staying with a friend. Ries's conjecture has greater probability. The work was published by the Bureau des Arts et d'Industrie in Vienna in 1807. (Society of Friends of Music, Vienna)

MARIE BIGOT DE MOROGES, NÉE KIÉNÉ (1786—1820)
Drawing made after an oil painting

This young woman, an outstanding pianist, had followed her husband to Vienna in 1804 when he was appointed librarian of Prince Rasumoffsky. When Beethoven once heard her play one of his sonatas, he said: "It is not exactly the character I meant to express, but go on, for if it is not all I, it is better than what I had in mind."

COMMENT BY RENÉ-PAUL BAILLOT, THE FRENCH PIANIST, WHO OWNED THE MANUSCRIPT OF THE SONATA, OPUS 57 FROM 1852 TILL HIS DEATH IN 1889

The note explains why most pages of the manuscript of the "Appassionata" show traces of raindrops (see the following pages). (Library, Paris Conservatory)

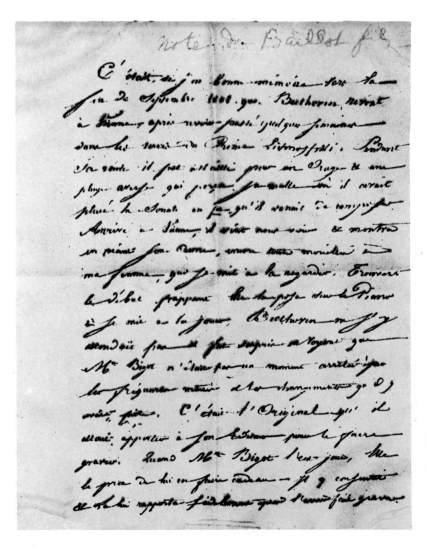

MANUSCRIPT PAGES OF THE "APPASSIONATA"   THE FIRST TWO PAGES OF THE ALLEGRO ASSAI

The upper right corner of the first page unfortunately is cut off. It probably bore Beethoven's signature or a comment which he himself removed later. It is worth remembering that "Appassionata" is not a term Beethoven selected. (Library, Paris Conservatory)

. . . OPUS 57, BY LUDWIG VAN BEETHOVEN
THE FIRST TWO PAGES OF THE ANDANTE CON MOTO

After the completion of the work Beethoven changed the beginning of the second movement and pasted a new version over the first and second staves. The manuscript came via Marie Bigot first to her husband and, in 1852, to the pianist René-Paul Baillot, who in turn bequeathed it to the "Bibliothèque du Conservatoire." (Library, Paris Conservatory)

The Countess, a cousin of the sisters Brunswick, in 1801 became Beethoven's pupil. He felt so passionately about her that he asked her to marry him. Her parents refused, which threw Beethoven into despair. Schindler and others believed Giulietta to be the "Immortal Beloved." However, the assertion is based on tenuous documentation.

GIULIETTA GUICCIARDI
Miniature, ivory

After Beethoven's death the portrait was found in his desk. (Bodmer, Zürich)

GIULIETTA GUICCIARDI
Portrait not signed

In 1803 she married Count Gallenberg, composer of ballets, who later became a theatrical director. The marriage was unhappy. (National Library, Vienna)

GIULIETTA, WIFE OF
COUNT ROBERT GALLENBERG
(1784—1856)
Marble by Schweikle
(Beethovenhaus, Bonn)

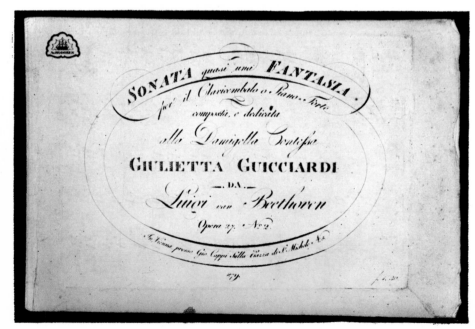

"SONATA QUASI UNA FANTASIA," C SHARP MINOR, OPUS 27, NO. 2, SO-CALLED "MOONLIGHT SONATA"
Title page with dedication to Countess Guicciardi

The Sonata was composed in 1801 and published by J. Cappi in Vienna in 1802. (van Hoboken, Ascona)

FIRST PAGE OF THE MANUSCRIPT OF THE MOONLIGHT SONATA

The first and the last page of this manuscript are lost. It begins with the third page, measure fourteen of the first movement. (Beethovenhaus, Bonn)

FIRST PAGE OF THE FINAL MOVEMENT OF THE MOONLIGHT SONATA

(Beethovenhaus, Bonn)

PAGES FROM ONE OF THE "CONVERSATION BOOKLETS"

That Beethoven's passion for Giulietta did not remain unreciprocated may be seen from these pages. This written conversation between the deaf teacher and Schindler, his pupil and biographer, took place in 1823 in a café in Vienna. Beethoven uses French in answering in order to divert indiscreet onlookers. The marriage of Giulietta had taken place twenty years before. (Former State Library, Berlin)

Here is the text: «*J'étois bien aimé d'elle, plus que jamais* [ne le fut] *son époux. Il étoit pourtant plutôt son amant, que moi. Mais, par elle, j'en apprenois de sa misère et je trouvois un homme de bien, qui me donnoit la somme de cinq cents* [florins] *pour le soulager. Il étoit toujours mon ennemi et c'étoit justement la raison que je* [lui] *fasse tout le bien que possible.*»

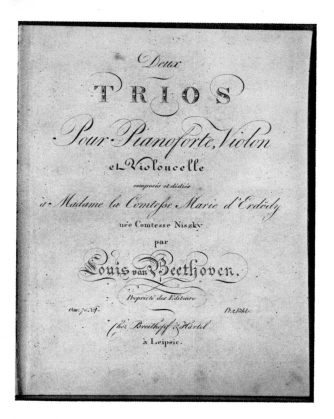

COUNTESS MARIE ERDÖDY, NÉE NISZKY (1779—1837)
Miniature, ivory

This portrait of his faithful friend—Beethoven called her his "father confessor"—was found in his desk after his death. In 1801 when despair overtook him while deafness was developing he had found refuge at the home of this warmhearted woman, who put him up in her farm Idlersee. Later he worked there frequently. — After a temporary discord followed by reconciliation the Countess in 1809 (when Beethoven had turned down an appointment by Jerome, King of Westphalia) saw to it that the agreement between Beethoven and Archduke Rudolf, Prince Lobkowitz and Prince Kinsky was concluded. (Bodmer, Zürich)

TWO TRIOS FOR PIANO, VIOLIN AND CELLO, OPUS 70
Title page with dedication to Countess Erdödy

These Trios were composed in 1808 and played in the Countess' drawing room, perhaps as a sign of their reconciliation. They were published by Breitkopf & Härtel in 1809. (Society of Friends of Music, Vienna)

TWO SONATAS FOR PIANO AND CELLO, OPUS 102
Title page of the original edition

Both sonatas were composed in 1815 and were published in 1819 at the same time by Simrock in Bonn and Artaria in Vienna. Beethoven had written on a copy of the manuscript: "Composed and dedicated to his friend Charles Neates." However, the Artaria edition bore the dedication: "Dedicated to the Countess Marie Erdödy, née Countess Niszky." (Society of Friends of Music, Vienna)

FRIEDRICH AUGUST KANNE (1778—1833)
Lithograph

Kanne, who first studied theology and medicine, later became a prolific composer and music critic. He was a protégé of Prince Lobkowitz and had friendly relations to Beethoven which sometimes were jeopardized by passionate controversy. (Society of Friends of Music, Vienna)

FERDINAND RIES (1784—1838)
Oil portrait

He was a son of Beethoven's friend Franz Ries, of Bonn, and was Beethoven's pupil from 1801 to 1805. After concert tours as pianist, he settled in London in 1813 and lived there till 1824. During that period Beethoven asked him frequently to represent his interests in Britain. Returning to Germany Ries became a conductor and continued his career as a diligent composer. In 1838 he published, together with Wegeler, the important "Biographical Notes on L. van Beethoven." (Beethovenhaus, Bonn)

CARL CZERNY (1791—1857)
Engraving by Blasius Höfel after Joseph Lanzedelly

At the age of ten Czerny became Beethoven's pupil and stayed with him for three years. Later Beethoven appointed him the teacher of his nephew Karl. Czerny was the first to play the E flat major Piano Concerto, opus 73—in Vienna in 1812. The work was dedicated to Archduke Rudolf. (National Library, Vienna)

JOHANN NEPOMUK HUMMEL (1778—1837)
Lithograph by Constans after Vigneron

In 1793 Hummel, after he had studied for two years with Mozart, and having concertized throughout Europe for five years, returned to Vienna where he worked with Albrechtsberger and Salieri. Beethoven who befriended him esteemed his brilliant playing highly. (Collection Cortot, Lausanne)

CARL FERDINAND AMENDA (1771—1836)
Oil painting by J. S. B. Grüne

This young theologian had come to Vienna from Kurland in 1798. He became one of Beethoven's best friends after the composer had heard him play the first violin part in one of his quartets. Their friendship was perfect even though Amenda left Vienna the following year. (Beethovenhaus, Bonn)

AUTOGRAPHED DEDICATION OF BEETHOVEN FOR HIS FRIEND C. F. AMENDA ON THE FIRST VIOLIN PART OF THE STRING QUARTET, OPUS 18, No. 1, F MAJOR

(Not Quartet No. 2 as erroneously indicated on the manuscript) The dedicatory text says: "Dear Amenda, take this Quartet as a small token of our friendship and whenever you play it for yourself remember the days we had together and at the same time how much devoted to you I was and will always be—your true and warm friend Ludwig van Beethoven. Vienna, 1799 on June the 25th." (Beethovenhaus, Bonn)

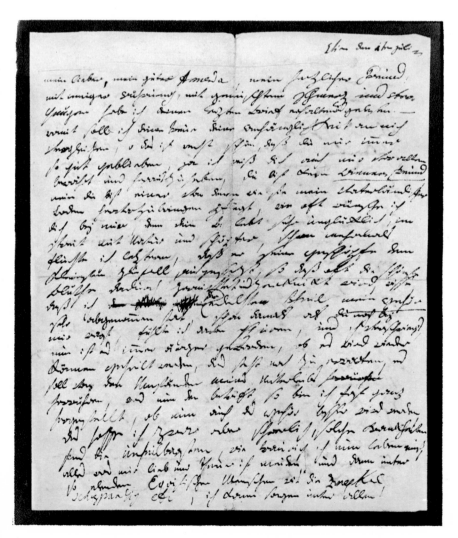

LETTER MANUSCRIPT OF BEETHOVEN TO C. F. AMENDA (Vienna, July 2?)

In this letter, probably from 1801, Beethoven mentions his beginning deafness for the first time and adds: "I ask you to consider the matter with my ear an important secret and to speak to no-one whatsoever about it . . ." (Bodmer, Zürich)

ABBÉ GEORG JOSEPH VOGLER (1749—1814)

Engraving by J. M. Schramm

In 1803 when his reputation as a composer, pianist and organist was firmly established, Vogler had come to Vienna and had shown great alertness in improvisations at the piano. Junkers, a critic of that time, stated in an equitable appraisal: "Beethoven, however, in addition to the virtuosity is more telling, more profound, more expressive—in one word he is more for the heart . . ." (Beethovenhaus, Bonn)

DANIEL STEIBELT (1765—1823)

Engraving by A. Quenedy

This famous piano virtuoso who had come to Vienna in 1800 had harvested rich laurels. In a sort of a musical tournament, however, in which he wanted to compete with Beethoven— it took place in the drawing rooms of the Count Fries—he lost out so obviously that he withdrew from the soirée before it ended. (National Library, Vienna)

ABBÉ JOSEPH GELINEK (1758—1825)

Engraving by C. F. Riedel after G. H. Lips

His manner of varying a theme was as famous as was his brilliant playing. After a competition with Beethoven he said: "A real Satan is in this young man. I have never heard anyone play like that, and on a theme furnished by me I have heard him improvise as not even Mozart could." (Beethovenhaus, Bonn)

JOSEPH WOELFL (1772—1812)

Engraving by Scheffner

This former pupil of Leopold Mozart enjoyed great popularity in Vienna both as a composer and pianist. Competing with Beethoven in a musical soirée in the home of the Baron von Wetzlar, he retained his prestige as a brilliant virtuoso whereas Beethoven emerged as the victor due to his improvisations and the profundity of his playing. (National Library, Vienna)

ANNOUNCEMENT OF THE CONCERT BEETHOVEN
GAVE IN VIENNA, AT THE NATIONAL COURT THEATER
ON APRIL 2, 1800 AT HIS OWN EXPENSE

The affair provided the Viennese public with an opportunity to acquaint itself not only with the great composer but with the conductor
and virtuoso. He played his Second Piano Concerto in B flat major,
opus 19, and also improvised, an activity which had always moved his
audiences. Then the Schuppanzigh ensemble performed the Septet,
opus 20, dedicated to the Empress Maria Theresia. Finally Beethoven
conducted his First Symphony in C, opus 21, which he had just completed. The success was unique. (Beethovenhaus, Bonn)

SEPTET FOR VIOLIN, VIOLA, CLARINET, HORN, BASSOON,
CELLO AND CONTRABASS IN E FLAT MAJOR, OPUS 20

Dedicatory page to Her Majesty, the Empress Maria Theresia. The
work was premiered April 2, 1800 and was published in 1802 by Hoffmeister, Vienna. (van Hoboken, Ascona)

MARIA CASENTINI

Made from an engraving

Maria Casentini between the years 1796 and 1801, and then again between 1803 and 1805, was one of the stars among the dancers of the Imperial Theater. The first performance of "The Creatures of Prometheus" was at her expense and she herself was cast in the role of the Statue which comes to life. (Society of Friends of Music, Vienna)

SALVATORE VIGANO (1769—1821)

Engraving by G. Scotto

Vigano, ballet master of the Viennese Theater, was responsible for the choreography of "The Creatures of Prometheus." He participated personally in the performance of this work. (National Library, Vienna)

ANNOUNCEMENT OF THE BALLET'S FIRST PERFORMANCE
CHOREOGRAPHY BY S. VIGANO, MUSIC BY BEETHOVEN

The master composed his first dramatic work on an allegorical subject by Salvatore Vigano. The performance originally announced for March 21, 1801, took place only on March 28th of that year, at the Court Theater of Vienna. (Society of Friends of Music, Vienna)

THE OLD BURGTHEATER, ALSO KNOWN AS "NATIONAL THEATER OF VIENNA"
Colored engraving

In this charming place the first performance of Beethoven's first stage work, "The Creatures of Prometheus," took place. (Historical Museum of the City of Vienna)

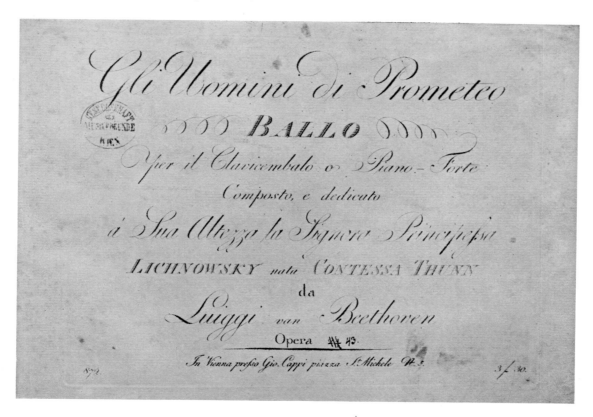

"THE CREATURES OF PROMETHEUS," OPUS 43, ORIGINALLY OPUS 24
Title page of the piano score with dedication to the Princess Lichnowsky

The work was composed in 1800 and 1801 and was first published as a piano transcription by Artaria, Vienna, and in 1802 by Cappi. The orchestral parts were published in 1804 but the whole score not until 1864. The critics considered the music as too scholarly. The composer himself wrote, on April 22, 1801, that the performance under the master of the ballet had not been entirely successful. It is certain that Vigano revised the ballet later for a performance in Milan, replacing certain parts composed by Beethoven with passages of other composers. (Society of Friends of Music, Vienna)

LUDWIG VAN BEETHOVEN
Portrait in oil signed Bock or Boch

Did this portrait inspire that of the painter Stainhauser which
is lost? Or is it the reverse? This question cannot be answered
with certainty. (Private Collection, Berlin)

LUDWIG VAN BEETHOVEN
After a gravure of C. F. Riedel

(Beethovenhaus, Bonn)

LUDWIG VAN BEETHOVEN
After a gravure by Johann Neidl

(Beethovenhaus, Bonn)

Both engravings are based on the lost painting by Stainhauser.

LUDWIG VAN BEETHOVEN (1803)
Miniature on ivory by Christian Horneman

This portrait was donated by Beethoven to his friend
Stephan von Breuning as token of a reconciliation. In the
accompanying letter (see below) Beethoven admits his
wrongdoing and asks his friend to forget what had
happened. (Bodmer, Zürich)

LUDWIG VAN BEETHOVEN (1804—05)
Portrait in oil by Willibord Joseph Mähler

This is the first of four portraits by this painter. It remained in
Beethoven's possession until he died and then went to his nephew
Karl. Today it belongs to one of his descendants. (Private Collec-
tion, Vienna)

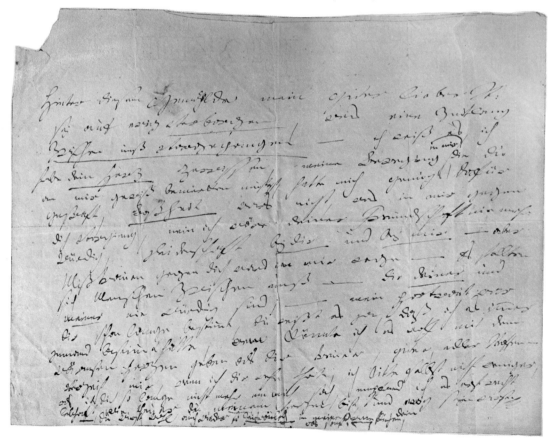

AUTOGRAPH OF BEETHOVEN TO STEPHAN VON BREUNING

This letter accompanied the miniature portrait above made by Horneman. (Bodmer, Zürich)

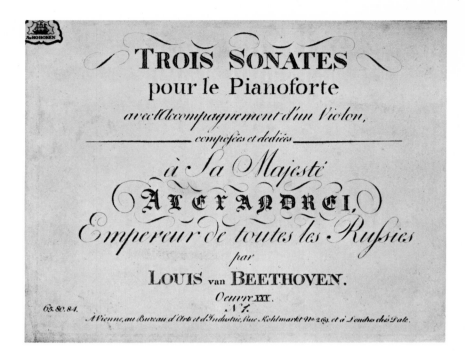

CZAR ALEXANDER I OF RUSSIA (1777—1825)

Oil portrait by Monnier

A music lover, the Czar had forgotten, however, to thank Beethoven for the dedication of opus 30, the Three Sonatas for Piano and Violin. Only in 1815 when Beethoven dedicated the Polonaise for Piano, opus 89 to Empress Elizabeth of Russia did he receive fifty ducats for the polonaise and additionally one hundred ducats for the mentioned sonatas. (Former Collection Stroganoff, Moscow)

THREE SONATAS FOR PIANO AND VIOLIN, OPUS 30

Dedicatory page for Czar Alexander I

Composed in 1802, the work was published in 1803 by the Bureau d'Arts et d'Industrie in Vienna. (van Hoboken, Ascona)

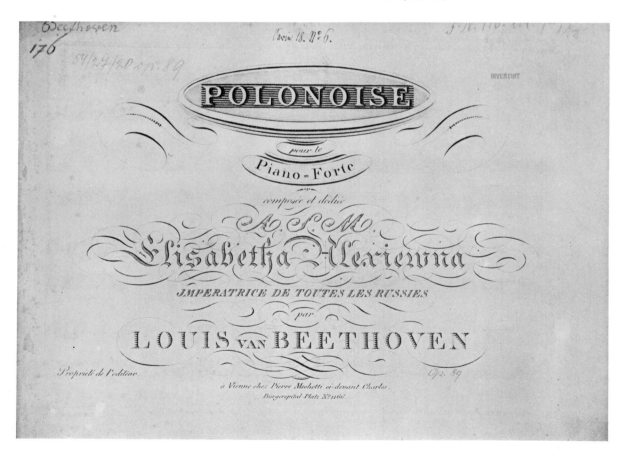

POLONAISE FOR PIANO, OPUS 89

Dedicatory page for the Empress Elizabeth of Russia

Composed in 1814, the work was published by Pierre Mechetti in Vienna in 1815. (Society of Friends of Music, Vienna)

LOUIS FERDINAND, PRINCE OF PRUSSIA (1772—1806)

Unsigned oil painting

The Prince, a nephew of Frederick the Great, fell in the battle of Saalfeld, October 10, 1806. He was a musician and composer of genuine talent and had unlimited admiration for Beethoven whose musical style influenced him. That Beethoven esteemed the Prince is proved by a remark made to the effect that "he plays piano not like a King or a Prince but like an excellent pianist"— Beethoven meant this to be a most flattering compliment. (National Gallery, Berlin)

PIANO CONCERTO NO. 3, C MINOR, OPUS 37

Title page with dedication for Louis Ferdinand, Prince of Prussia

Composed in 1800, the concerto was premiered by Beethoven at the Theater an der Wien on April 5, 1803. On this occasion he also conducted for the first time his Second Symphony, opus 36, and his oratorio "Christ on Mount Olive," opus 85. The C minor Piano Concerto was published by the Bureau d'Arts et d'Industrie in 1804. (Society of Friends of Music, Vienna)

HEILIGENSTADT

Water color by Tobias Raulino

Beethoven, whose deafness dated back to 1800 and grew gradually worse, was overcome by fear and shyness. He passed the summer of 1802 in this little village hoping to find recovery from his suffering. The latter failed to come even though the period itself is characterized by the creation of most important compositions. (Historical Museum of the City of Vienna)

THE CHURCH OF HEILIGENSTADT

Colored engraving by L. Janscha

During his sojourn in Heiligenstadt in 1802, Beethoven composed, at least in part, the Six Piano Variations, opus 34, the Fifteen Variations and Fugue for Piano, opus 35, on a theme from "Prometheus," and above all his Second Symphony, D major, opus 36. (Historical Museum of the City of Vienna)

TITLE PAGE OF THE "RÉPERTOIRE DES CLAVECINISTES"

J. G. Naegeli of Zürich, a Swiss publisher, at the beginning of the nineteenth century published a collection of new works under this title, and was the first to publish, in the fifth volume of this collection, the piano sonatas, opus 31, Nos. 1 and 2 by Beethoven. (van Hoboken, Ascona)

TWO SONATAS FOR PIANO, OPUS 31, NOS. 1 AND 2

Title page of the first edition published by J. G. Naegeli in Zürich, 1803

Naegeli, knowing Beethoven's character but insufficiently, had the unhappy idea of modifying Beethoven's version in his own fashion according to his own taste. To the first Allegro of the sonata in G major he added, on page 9, four measures. When Beethoven discovered this arbitrariness he was beside himself and asked his pupil Ries immediately to contact the publisher Simrock in Bonn so he would publish a new edition of the two sonatas. The title page of the new edition was supposed to carry the words: «Edition très correcte.» (van Hoboken, Ascona)

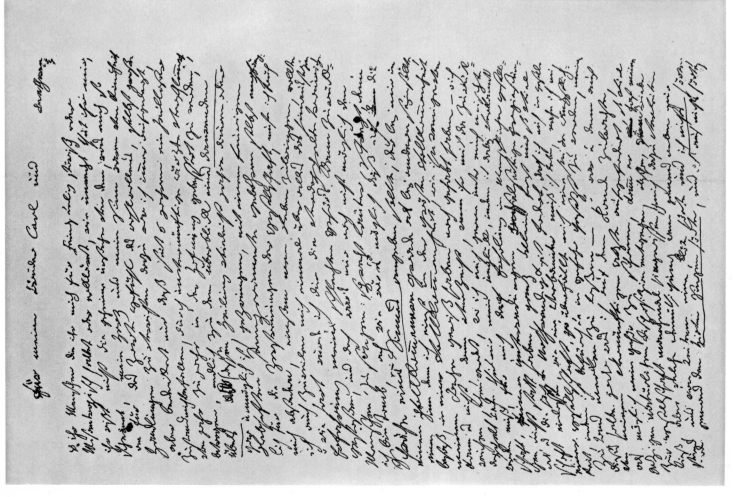

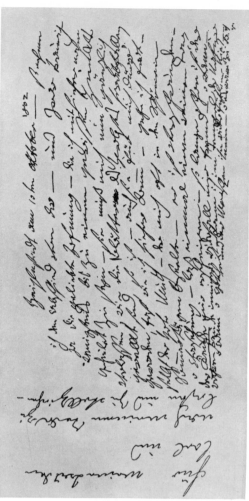

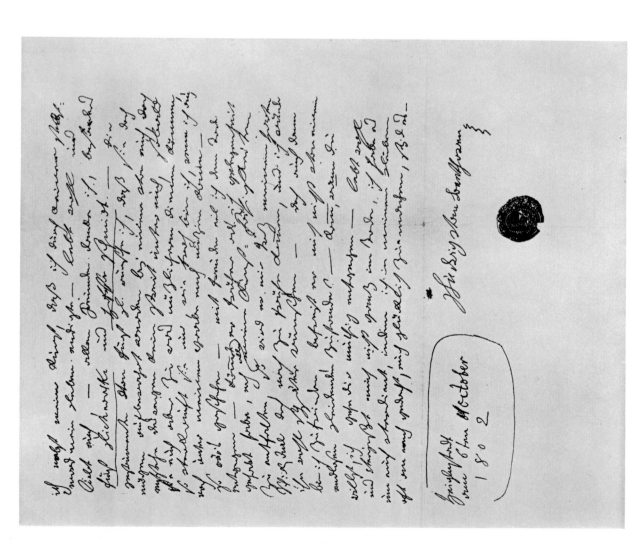

The Heiligenstadt Testament, October 6, 1802

When Beethoven felt that despite all efforts to regain health his deafness made but faster progress, he suffered a nervous attack and even harbored thoughts of suicide. Although not attempting it, he expected the worst and for the benefit of his brothers wrote this famous document usually referred to as the "Heiligenstadt Testament."

IN THE PARK OF SCHÖNBRUNN NEAR VIENNA

Colored engraving by J. Siegler after L. Janscha

Beethoven loved to walk in this park which gave him many an inspiration for his compositions. Here, for instance, he worked on his oratorio "Christ on Mount Olive" between 1802 and 1803, and on his opera "Fidelio" in 1804. (Historical Museum of the City of Vienna)

THE "WHITE SWAN" TAVERN AT THE NEUMARKT OF VIENNA

Water color by Emil Hütter

As early as 1796 Beethoven was a steady guest in this tavern. Here he had his rendezvous, for instance with his faithful friend Nicolas Zmeskall of Domanowetz. (Historical Museum of the City of Vienna)

ST. PETER AND ST. PETER'S SQUARE, VIENNA
Colored engraving by Carl Schütz

Returning from Heiligenstadt in 1802, Beethoven took lodgings at "St. Peter's Square" near the police station in which a company of mounted police was housed. One recognizes, at the right, the entrance to the station. (Historical Museum of the City of Vienna)

"CHRIST ON MOUNT OLIVE," OPUS 85
Title page of the piano score

On the title page of the original edition the dedication, in Beethoven's hand, says: "To my respected friend Frau Toni von Brentano, née von Birkenstock, by the author." See page 138. The oratorio was composed in 1803. Breitkopf & Härtel published the first orchestral score and the piano reduction in October, 1811. (Beethovenhaus, Bonn)

RUDOLF KREUTZER (1766—1831)
Engraving by C. T. Riedel after A. P. Vincent

Kreutzer, composer and violinist, later became the conductor of the orchestra of the Paris Opera. In 1798 he came to Vienna in the entourage of Bernadotte. Here he made Beethoven's acquaintance, and the latter found him congenial and after his departure from Vienna maintained correspondence with him. On October 4, 1804, Beethoven wrote to the publisher Simrock: "This man Kreutzer is a good and amiable man who has given me much pleasure during his sojourn here. His unpretentiousness and simple attitude please me more than the exterior and interior of most virtuosos. Since my Sonata is written for a first class violinist it seems indicated to dedicate the work to him." However, Kreutzer did not seem to esteem this honor too highly, as is evidenced by an ironic declaration of Berlioz in his "Musical Voyage in Germany and Italy," published 1844, where he writes: "Beethoven had dedicated one of his loftiest sonatas for piano and violin to Kreutzer; one must admit that this dedication was justified. The more incredible is it that the famous violinist never saw fit to perform the composition." (Beethovenhaus, Bonn)

SONATA FOR PIANO AND VIOLIN, IN A MAJOR, OPUS 47, THE SO-CALLED "KREUTZERSONATE"
Dedicatory page to Rudolf Kreutzer, the violinist

Bridgetower, a violinist in the services of the Prince of Wales, gave two concerts in Vienna in the Hall of the "Augarten," May 17 and 24, 1803. At Bridgetower's request Beethoven undertook the writing of the A major Sonata, but there was little time and he could finish only the first Allegro and the Andante with Variations. In the concert of May 17th the two musicians played these first two movements of the Sonata and finished their performance with the last movement of the Sonata, opus 30, No. 1. The real Finale was composed later. The work itself, published by Simrock in Bonn in 1805, was finally dedicated to Kreutzer since the composer had had a serious falling out with Bridgetower. (Society of Friends of Music, Vienna)

SONATA FOR PIANO, C MAJOR, OPUS 53, BY LUDWIG VAN BEETHOVEN
Title page with dedication to Count Ferdinand von Waldstein

The work was composed 1803—04 and published in 1805 by the Bureau d'Arts et d'Industrie, Vienna. With this dedication of one of his most important piano sonatas Beethoven discharged an old indebtedness to one of his first benefactors in Bonn. (van Hoboken, Ascona)

FIRST PAGE OF THE MANUSCRIPT OF THE PIANO SONATA, OPUS 53

At the end of this manuscript, Beethoven inscribed: "Sonata grande da L. van Beethoven," then he crossed out the words "da L. van Beethoven." On the right margin a note in his hand: "NB where it says ped, the total damper, both a little bass and discant, is lifted. 0 means that it is dropped again." This manuscript for a long time belonged to the branch of the Counts within the Waldstein family of Prague. (Bodmer, Zürich)

TITLE PAGE OF THE AUTOGRAPHED SCORE OF SYMPHONY No. 3 IN E FLAT MAJOR, OPUS 55, SO-CALLED "EROICA"

The autograph of this Symphony has disappeared. The manuscript of which two pages are reproduced here is a copy used by Beethoven. In the upper right corner of the title page there is his entry: "Nb 1. Into the first violin part the other instruments are partly to be entered." Below the title by the hand of the copyist: "Sinfonia grande intitolata Bonaparte. 1804 in August by Signor Louis van Beethoven." The words "intitolata Bonaparte" were violently struck out by the author when learning that the "First Consul" for whom he had harbored great admiration had made himself Emperor.—At the bottom, also from Beethoven's hand: "NB The third horn is so written that it may be blown by either a primario or secundario." (Society of Friends of Music, Vienna)

PAGE FROM THE FINALE OF A MANUSCRIPT SCORE OF THE "EROICA"

On this page, written by a copyist, we find numerous corrections made by Beethoven himself in his own hand with ink and with red pencil. After the work had been played several times in the drawing rooms of Prince Lobkowitz, it was first publicly performed on April 7, 1805 under the composer's direction. (Society of Friends of Music, Vienna)

THE THIRD SYMPHONY IN E FLAT MAJOR, OPUS 55, SO-CALLED "EROICA"

Orchestral parts (1806), title page with dedication to Prince Lobkowitz; *orchestral score (1809),* first page with the note "composed to glorify a hero's death."

This monumental work broke with the traditional style of the classical symphony. Composed in the years 1803—04, it was published in its first edition (orchestral parts) by the Bureau d'Arts et d'Industrie in Vienna. Three years later the publishers Cianchettini & Sperati, London, published the first edition of the orchestral score (1809). (van Hoboken, Ascona; British Museum, London)

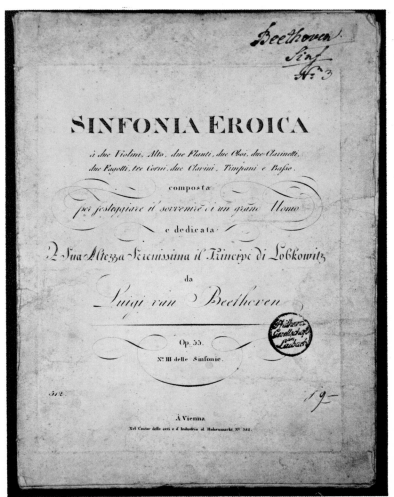

EMANUEL SCHIKANEDER (1751—1812)

Engraving by Löschenkohl

Schikaneder who as an actor belonged to the Burgtheater, in 1788 assumed the direction of the Freihaustheater of Vienna. He is the author of the libretto of Mozart's "Magic Flute," the greatest success experienced by this theater. In June, 1801, he assumed the direction of the Theater an der Wien which had just been built. He offered Beethoven an apartment in the new theater building and commissioned him with the composition of his libretto: "Vesta's Fire." However, Beethoven, after a brief start and a sketch of the first scenes of the opera, withdrew from the commission. (Mozart Museum, Salzburg)

THE IMPERIAL AND ROYAL THEATER AN DER WIEN

Colored engraving

From the beginning of 1805 Beethoven lived in the rooms offered by Schikaneder. The Theater an der Wien saw in succession the premières of several of Beethoven's large works: the "Eroica" on April 7, 1805, "Fidelio" on November 20 of that year, the Violin Concerto on December 23, 1806, and on the 22nd of December 1808, the Fifth Symphony and the "Pastoral" Symphony plus the "Fantasy for Piano, Chorus and Orchestra," opus 80, in part under the personal direction of the composer. (Historical Museum of the City of Vienna)

JOSEPH SONNLEITHNER (1766—1835)

Oil painting by Alois Karner

When Baron von Braun succeeded Schikaneder in the direction of the Theater an der Wien in 1804, he asked Beethoven to write an opera for the theater. The composer's choice was a French work "Leonore" or "Conjugal Love" by J. N. Bouilly, and the translation and arrangement of the libretto were entrusted to Sonnleithner, the Secretary of Court, who transformed the subject matter into a three act drama. Beethoven, enthused over the idea of glorifying marital love, went to work without delay. (Private Collection, Vienna)

GEORG FRIEDRICH TREITSCHKE
(1776—1842)

Lithograph by Joseph Kriehuber

First an actor, then a dramaturgist, Treitschke was the director of the Viennese Opera when "Fidelio" was premiered there. After the failure of 1805 and the demisuccess of 1806 he changed the libretto of the opera for the performances of 1814. (Beethovenhaus, Bonn)

IGNAZ VON SEYFRIED (1776—1841)

After a lithograph of Joseph Kriehuber

The former pupil of Mozart and Albrechtsberger, Seyfried was director of the orchestra at the Theater an der Wien from 1798 to 1828. During the rehearsals for "Fidelio" which he conducted on March 29 and April 10, he made Beethoven's acquaintance and a quasi-friendship developed. (Beethovenhaus, Bonn)

Notwithstanding the occupation of Vienna by Napoleon (November 13, 1805) and the deplorable circumstances created by the events, the first performance of "Fidelio" took place November 20, 1805 at the Theater an der Wien. The outcome was not commensurate with the expectations of the composer and his friends, and after three performances the work disappeared from the schedules. — Convinced of the value of this work, Beethoven had the libretto revised and shortened by his friend Stephan von Breuning. He also made changes in the score and modified the title to read "Leonore or the Triumph of Conjugal Love," an opera in two (in lieu of three) acts. On March 29, 1806 the opera was again performed, in this revision. However, after two performances Beethoven quarreled with the management and withdrew the opera. (National Library, Vienna)

FRITZ DEMMER

Lithograph

This tenor sang Florestan in the première of "Fidelio" (National Library, Vienna)

ANNA MILDER-HAUPTMANN (1785—1838)

Water color by Perger

This famous Viennese singer sang the role of Leonore in the first performance. (National Library, Vienna)

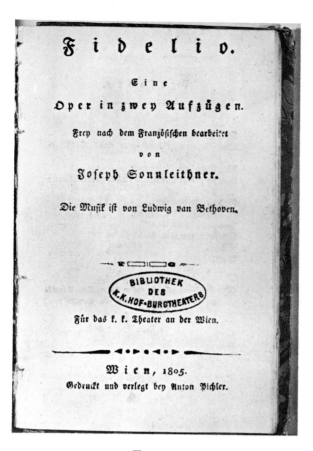

FIDELIO
LIBRETTO BY JOSEPH SONNLEITHNER

Title page of the first edition published by Anton Pichler,
Vienna, 1805. (National Library, Vienna)

LEONORE OR THE TRIUMPH OF
CONJUGAL LOVE,
LIBRETTO BY J. SONNLEITHNER, REVISED
BY STEPHAN VON BREUNING

Title page of the second edition, published by Anton
Pichler in Vienna, 1806. (Society of Friends of Music,
Vienna)

NAPOLEON AND HIS TROOPS ENTERING VIENNA
Engraving by Le Beau, after Naudet

After the capitulation of Ulm Napoleon marched toward Vienna and captured it November 13, 1805. On December 2
he destroyed the Russian and Austrian armies at Austerlitz in Moravia which had been led by Czar Alexander I and
Emperor Franz II. On December 26 of that year the peace treaty of Pressburg was concluded. Through it, the States
of Venice became part of the Kingdom of Italy and various members of Napoleon's family ascended the thrones of
Westphalia, Spain, Naples and Holland. In the year 1809 Vienna was occupied by Napoleon for the second time.
(Historical Museum of the City of Vienna)

AUTOGRAPH OF THE MARCH FROM FIDELIO (1804—05)

In the first version of the opera (three acts), as it was performed in 1805, this March figured at the beginning of the second act. At the bottom of the page Beethoven says: "Where the measures are empty, rests are to be made." (Bodmer, Zürich)

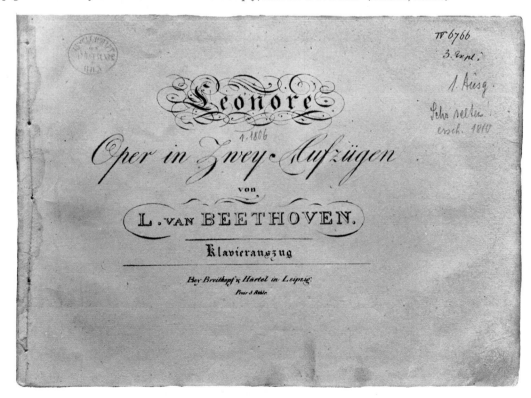

LEONORE (FIDELIO) SCORE FOR PIANO AND VOICE

Title page of the first edition for piano and voice

Published in 1810 by Breitkopf & Härtel in Leipzig. This arrangement of the version of 1806 does not contain the Overture Leonore No. 3, nor the aria of Rocco, nor the Finale. (Society of Friends of Music, Vienna)

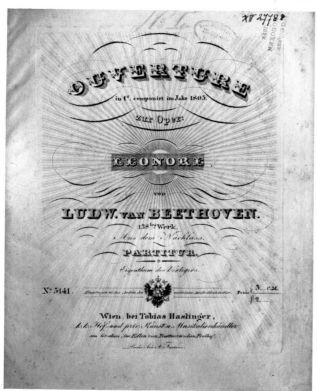

"Leonore Overture No. 1," C major
Title page of the orchestral score

This Overture, composed in 1805 and not too highly esteemed by Beethoven, was first performed with a small orchestra at Prince Lichnowsky's salon. It found no acclaim with the listeners and Beethoven withdrew it. Rediscovered after his death, however, it was published by Haslinger in Vienna in 1838. (Society of Friends of Music, Vienna)

"Leonore Overture No. 2," C major
Title page of the orchestral score

The work dates from the autumn of 1805 and was used for the performance of "Fidelio" on November 20, 1805 and the two succeeding performances. Then it disappeared and was printed only in 1842, by Breitkopf & Härtel in Leipzig. (van Hoboken, Ascona)

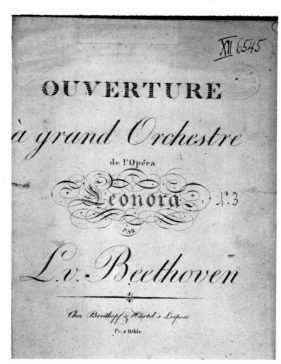

"Leonore Overture No. 3," C major
Title page of the orchestral parts

This Overture was completed in March, 1806 and used for the performances of March 29 and April 10, 1806. The first edition of the orchestral parts was published in 1810 by Breitkopf & Härtel, but the first edition of the score appeared not before 1828. (Society of Friends of Music, Vienna)

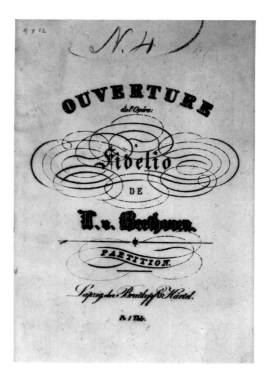

"Overture to Fidelio," E major
Title page of the orchestral score published in 1828

This Overture was composed in May, 1814 for the revised score of "Fidelio" and was heard in the performance of May 26, 1814. For the performance of May 23, however, in other words, three days earlier, the Overture to "The Ruins of Athens" was played since the "Fidelio" Overture had not been completed. (van Hoboken, Ascona)

THE THIRD AND LAST VERSION OF "FIDELIO"

In the spring of 1814 Johann Michael Vogl, Schubert's well known friend, together with two of his colleagues of the Theater at the Kärntnerthor, addressed himself to Beethoven with the request that they be permitted to perform "Fidelio" at their expense. Beethoven once more revised his work, the text of which had already been revised by Treitschke. Above all, he composed a fourth overture, the "Overture to Fidelio." In this final form which is that known throughout the world, the work when performed on May 23, 1814 and with all subsequent performances had an enormous success.

POSTER FOR THE PERFORMANCE OF "FIDELIO"
AT THE THEATER AT THE KÄRNTNERTHOR, MAY 23, 1814
(National Library, Vienna)

KARL WEINMÜLLER (1764—1828)
Engraving by David Weiss after C. Mahnke

Weinmüller, one of the stars of the Vienna Opera, was a touching Rocco.

JOHANN MICHAEL VOGL (1768—1840)
After a lithograph of Joseph Kriehuber

Vogl, united with Schubert in an inseparable friendship, was cast in the role of Pizarro in 1814. (Beethovenhaus, Bonn)

PIZARRO WANTS TO STAB FLORESTAN,
SCENE FROM THE SECOND ACT OF "FIDELIO"
Engraving by V. R. Grüner

This print is found in the edition of the "Wiener Hoftheater-
Taschenbuch" of 1815. (National Library, Vienna)

IGNAZ MOSCHELES (1794—1870)
Lithography by Brandt

This eminent pianist who already at the age of fourteen
had made public appearances worked in Vienna under
the direction of Albrechtsberger and Salieri. In 1814
Beethoven entrusted to him the task of writing a piano
score of "Fidelio." (Collection Cortot, Lausanne)

CRITIQUE OF A "FIDELIO"
PERFORMANCE

In Number 63 of the Theater Jour-
nal of May 28, 1814 the chronicler
gives an enthusiastic résumé of the
performance of May 23, 1814. (City
Library, Vienna)

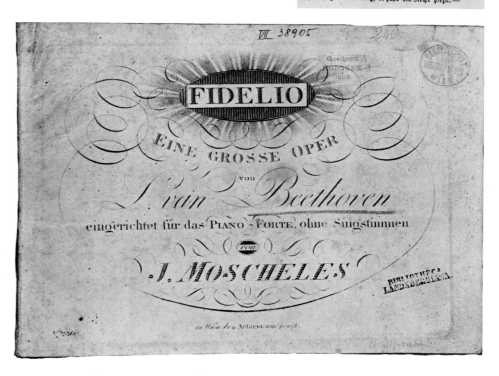

PIANO SCORE OF "FIDELIO" ARRANGED BY MOSCHELES

This arrangement of the third and last version of Beethoven's opera was published, in August
1814, by Artaria & Cie., Vienna. (Society of Friends of Music, Vienna)

THERESE VON MALFATTI (1792—1851)
Pastel

She was the daughter of a rich landowner and the niece of the well known Dr. Malfatti, a physician who for a time treated Beethoven. She became acquainted with the composer in her father's home to which Beethoven had been introduced by a mutual friend, Ignaz von Gleichenstein. Beethoven fell in love with her and asked for her hand. The rejection proved a tragedy for him. (Gleichenstein Collection)

BARON IGNAZ VON GLEICHENSTEIN
(1778—1828)
Lithograph

The Baron was part of the Imperial administration and in 1797 became Beethoven's friend. His gay and captivating manner made him a treasured and a judicious adviser to the composer. He married Anna von Malfatti, Therese's sister. (Gleichenstein Collection)

SONATA FOR PIANO AND VIOLONCELLO, A MAJOR, OPUS 69
Title page with dedication to Baron von Gleichenstein

The magnificent A major Sonata was dedicated to his friend who was an extraordinary cellist. It was a sign of Beethoven's gratitude. Composed in 1807—08, it was published in 1809 by Breitkopf & Härtel in Leipzig. The motto placed by the composer at the beginning of his composition "Inter lacrimas et luctum" (in tears and sadness) is in reference to the still raging war. (Society of Friends of Music, Vienna)

LUDWIG VAN BEETHOVEN (CA. 1808)
Pencil drawing by Ludwig Schnorr von Carolsfeld

Under the portrait an unknown hand has written: "From the old director Schnorr von Carolsfeld, of Dresden, in the year 1808 or 1809 in a sketch book of the Malfatti family in Munich. In the possession of Frau von Gleichenstein, née Malfatti in Freiburg im Breisgau." (Gleichenstein Collection)

LUDWIG VAN BEETHOVEN (1806)
Portrait in oil by Isidor Neugass

This painting by the Viennese painter Neugass was a commission of Prince Lichnowsky. It has only small significance because it idealizes the model too strongly. (Collection Lichnowsky, Grätz)

LUDWIG VAN BEETHOVEN (1805?)
Oil painting, unsigned

This portrait was a commission by Count Franz von Brunswick and is probably from the workshop of Neugass. (Marchesa Capponi, Florence)

119

FIRST PAGE FROM THE MANUSCRIPT OF THE CONCERTO FOR VIOLIN AND ORCHESTRA, D MAJOR, OPUS 61

Beethoven, who had entrusted the first performance of the Violin Concerto to the violinist Clement, wrote at the beginning of the manuscript "Concerto par Clemenza pour Clement, primo Violino e Direttore al Theatro a Vienna, dal L. v. Bthn. 1806." The orchestral parts were published in 1808 by the Bureau d'Arts et d'Industrie in Vienna and in Pesth yet the score was not published before 1861 by C. F. Peters in Leipzig and Berlin. In 1807 Beethoven transcribed his work for "piano and orchestra." The original version of the Violin Concerto was dedicated to his friend Stephan von Breuning and the transcription for piano and orchestra to Julie von Breuning. (National Library, Vienna)

FRANZ JOSEF CLEMENT (1780—1842)
Engraving by H. Hessell (1789)

Born in Vienna, Clement like Mozart was a prodigy both as a violinist and composer. Beethoven had him perform his only Violin Concerto on December 23, 1806. Unhappily the artist later became a drunkard after he had been a conductor in Vienna and Prague. (National Library, Vienna)

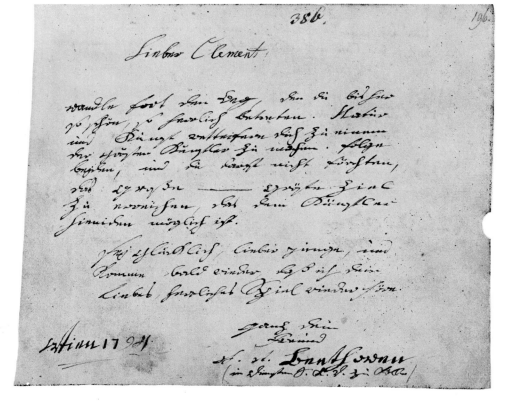

PAGE FROM AN ALBUM OF FRANZ CLEMENT
WITH AUTOGRAPH OF BEETHOVEN

The entry says: "Dear Clement, continue on the road which till now you have so magnificently travelled. Nature and art compete in their endeavor to make you one of the greatest artists. Follow both and you need not fear to achieve the greatest aim an artist can achieve in this world. Be happy, dear boy, and come back soon so I can listen again to your magnificent playing. Your friend, L. v. Beethoven, Vienna, 1794." Beethoven was twenty-four, Clement only fourteen. (National Library, Vienna)

FIRST PAGE FROM THE AUTOGRAPH OF THE "CORIOLAN" OVERTURE, OPUS 62

At the beginning of the manuscript Beethoven's entry: "Ouverture (zum Trauerspiel Coriolan) composta de L. v. Beethoven 1807." The words in parentheses were later erased by him. The Overture was performed in one of the so-called "amateur" concerts in Vienna, December, 1807. (Beethovenhaus, Bonn)

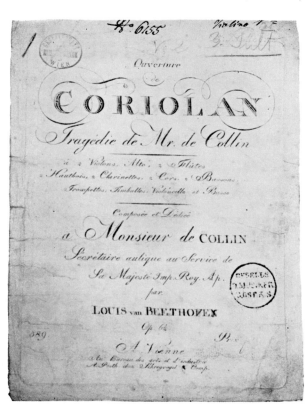

"CORIOLAN" OVERTURE, OPUS 62

Dedicatory page to H. J. von Collin

Written in 1807, the work was published in 1808 by the Bureau d'Arts et d'Industrie in Vienna. (Society of Friends of Music, Vienna)

HEINRICH JOSEPH VON COLLIN (1772—1811)

Engraving by J. F. Bolt after J. Lange

He had originally furnished two librettos, Macbeth and Brada-mante, the composition of which Beethoven refused. He was finally successful with "Coriolan" in that the composer decided to write his famous Overture for it. (Beethovenhaus, Bonn)

ANDRÉ CYRILLOWITSCH, PRINCE RASUMOFFSKY (1752—1836)
Miniature on ivory

The Prince had arrived in Vienna 1790 and was the ambassador of the Czar at the Court of Vienna, a position which he held from 1792 till 1809 with but a short interruption. He was responsible for the Austrian-Russian treaty against Napoleon in 1812. His marvelous palace was the center of the high aristocracy. A musician himself and an enthusiastic admirer of Beethoven's work, he founded in 1808 a string quartet in which he himself was a second violinist and in which he employed the famous Schuppanzigh whom he had enticed away from Prince Lichnowsky. This ensemble was at Beethoven's disposal for the performance of his chamber music. During the time of the Congress of Vienna, Rasumoffsky gave feasts of unheard-of luxury. (Former Collection A., Moscow)

THE RASUMOFFSKY PALACE IN VIENNA
Water color by E. Gurk

In this fabulous palace the Prince had collected art works of enormous value. His receptions exceeded in splendor everything the Viennese aristocracy had heretofore experienced, particularly in 1814 while the Congress was in session. The palace was destroyed by fire during the night of December 30, 1814. (Historical Museum of the City of Vienna)

AUTOGRAPH OF THE STRING QUARTET, C MAJOR, OPUS 59, NO. 3

At the head of the manuscript Beethoven's entry: "Quartetto terzo da Luigi van Beethoven." The three quartets opus 59 dedicated to Prince Rasumoffsky were composed 1805—06 but published in 1808 by the Bureau d'Arts et d'Industrie, Vienna. (Beethovenhaus, Bonn)

COVER OF THE AUTOGRAPH OF STRING QUARTET, OPUS 59, NO. 3

This precious manuscript of one of the three string quartets dedicated to Prince Rasumoffsky became part of the collection of the Beethovenhaus in Bonn in 1904. It is bound in red velvet with title and corners in gold-plated metal, enameled and with multi-colored pearls (polychromes). (Beethovenhaus, Bonn)

PRINCE NICOLAUS ESTERHÁZY (1765—1833)
Colored engraving

Just as had his father, Prince Nicolaus entrusted Haydn with the direction of his orchestra. Haydn introduced Beethoven to the Prince who received him most cordially. To the Princess Esterházy Beethoven dedicated his opus 45, the "Three Grand Marches for Piano, four hands." (National Library, Vienna)

C MAJOR MASS FOR FOUR VOICES, CHORUS AND ORCHESTRA, OPUS 86

Prince Esterházy in 1807 commissioned Beethoven to write a Mass for the anniversary of the Princess. This gave Beethoven an opportunity to treat the liturgical text in a personal and novel manner and therefore indicated the road that later led to his magnificent "Missa Solemnis." However, used to traditional music, the Prince was not pleased with the work the execution of which, under the composer's direction, also left much to be desired. As a result the relations between Beethoven and the Prince deteriorated and ended entirely when, in 1812, the Mass was published with the dedication to Prince Kinsky. (Society of Friends of Music, Vienna)

FIRST PAGE OF THE AUTOGRAPH OF THE FIFTH SYMPHONY IN C MINOR, OPUS 67

At the head of the manuscript Beethoven noted with red pencil: "Sinfonia da L. v. Beethoven." The entry has become almost illegible. Below the second measure the composer noted with ink: "Flauti, oboe, clarinetti, fagotti, corni, tutti obligati." The Symphony in C minor was composed in the period between 1804 and 1808 and first heard on December 22, 1808 at the Theater an der Wien under the composer's direction. The occasion was a concert entirely devoted to works of Beethoven. (Former State Library, Berlin)

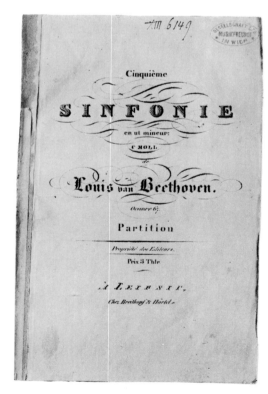

FIFTH SYMPHONY IN C MINOR, OPUS 67

Orchestral parts   *Score*

Title page with dedication to Prince Lobkowitz and Count   Title page
Rasumoffsky. (van Hoboken, Ascona)   (Society of Friends of Music, Vienna)

The first edition of the Fifth Symphony (orchestral parts only) was published by Breitkopf & Härtel in Leipzig in 1809. Only in 1826, however, did the same publishers release the orchestral score.

AUTOGRAPH OF THE "SYMPHONIE PASTORALE" No. 6, F MAJOR, OPUS 68

First page of the first movement

At the head of the score from Beethoven's hand: "Sinfonia 6ta da Luigi van Beethoven. Allegro ma non troppo. Pleasant, gay sentiments such as are awakened in the human being when arriving in the country." On the right margin half way down the composer repeats the word "awaken." At the bottom of the page his note "P. S. the German titles such as not too fast, sixth symphony by Ludwig van Beethoven—write them all into the first violin part." (Beethovenhaus, Bonn)

PAGE FROM THE AUTOGRAPH OF THE "PASTORAL SYMPHONY"

One of the last pages of the second movement

This concerns the famous passage evoking the song of the birds. At the bottom of the page Beethoven notes: "P. S. write the words nightingale, quail, cuckoo, into the first flutes, the first oboe, the first and second clarinets just as here in the score." (Beethovenhaus, Bonn)

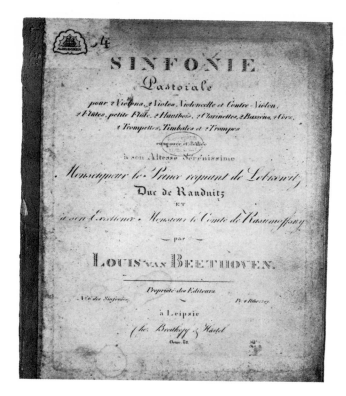

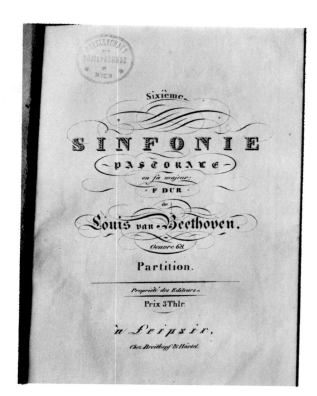

THE "PASTORAL SYMPHONY" No. 6, F MAJOR, OPUS 68

Orchestral parts
Title page with dedication to Prince Lobkowitz and Count Rasumoffsky
(van Hoboken, Ascona)

Score
Title page
(Society of Friends of Music, Vienna)

The work was completed in 1808 during his sojourn in Heiligenstadt and is an incomparable testimony to his sensitivity to nature. The first public performance took place December 22, 1808 under the composer's direction at the Theater an der Wien. In 1809 Breitkopf & Härtel, Leipzig, published the symphony, i.e., only the orchestral parts, and the score was released by the same house in 1826. In one of his notebooks Beethoven comments on this symphony: "Those who have an idea of country life will know what the author wishes without many explanations."

BEETHOVEN WORKING ON HIS
"PASTORAL SYMPHONY"

Colored lithograph from the Almanac of the Society of Music of Zürich, published in 1834

Speaking about the valley of Nussdorf near Vienna, Beethoven said to his biographer Schindler: "There I wrote the 'Episode at the Brook' and the goldhammers up there, the quails, nightingales and cuckoos around helped me compose." (Bodmer, Zürich)

THE THEATER AN DER WIEN VIEWED FROM THE JÄGERGASSE
Colored engraving

Three days before Christmas 1808 Beethoven presented a "Grand Academy" with his most recent works. Under his direction the "Pastoral Symphony" and the Fifth Symphony were heard whereupon the master himself played his Fourth Piano Concerto and the piano part of the Fantasy, opus 80. (National Library, Vienna)

THE THEATER AN DER WIEN
Colored engraving

This is the place where the famous concert of December 22, 1808 took place. The first performances of the "Eroica," the "Fidelio" and the Violin Concerto had also been given here. (Historical Museum of the City of Vienna)

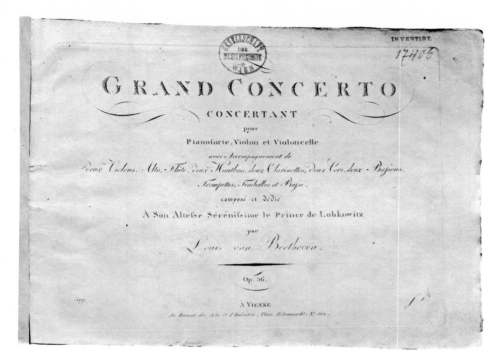

CONCERTO FOR PIANO, VIOLIN, VIOLONCELLO
WITH THE ACCOMPANIMENT OF THE ORCHESTRA,
C MAJOR, OPUS 56

Title page with dedication to Prince Lobkowitz

The triple concerto was composed in 1803—04 and published
in 1807 by the Bureau d'Arts et d'Industrie in Vienna. (Society of Friends of Music, Vienna)

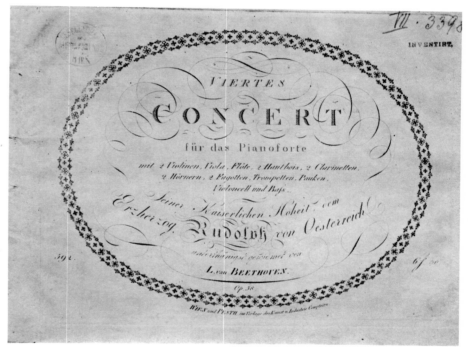

PIANO CONCERTO No. 4, G MAJOR, OPUS 58

Title page with dedication to Archduke Rudolf of Austria

Composed in 1805—06, the concerto was played by Beethoven in March 1807 at a concert in
the palace of Prince Lobkowitz and was published in 1808 by the Bureau d'Arts et d'Industrie
in Vienna. (Society of Friends of Music, Vienna)

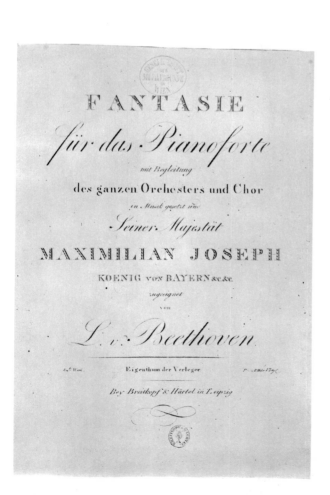

FANTASY FOR PIANO, CHORUS AND ORCHESTRA, OPUS 80

Title page with dedication to Maximilian Josef, King of Bavaria

The work, written in 1808, for the first time in musical history uses the human voice like an
instrument and thereby provides a model for the Finale of the Ninth Symphony. The Fantasy
was published by Breitkopf & Härtel in Leipzig in 1811. (Society of Friends of Music, Vienna)

PRINCE FERDINAND KINSKY (1781—1812)
Lithograph by Joseph Kriehuber

He was one of Beethoven's most sympathetic patrons and in 1809 together with Archduke Rudolf and the Prince Lobkowitz offered Beethoven a fixed annual grant which persuaded him to turn down the offer made by Kassel and to remain in Vienna. (National Library, Vienna)

PRINCESS CAROLINE MARIE KINSKY
NÉE VON KERPEN (1782—1841)
Lithograph by Kriehuber after Ender

The composer dedicated to his patron's wife the Six Songs, opus 75, the Three Songs, opus 83, as well as his opus 94 "An die Hoffnung." (National Library, Vienna)

THE KINSKY PALACE IN VIENNA
Drawing by Salomon Kleiner

The brilliant Prince Kinsky who had participated in the battles against Napoleon did not die in battle, but at the age of thirty-one was fatally injured as a result of being thrown from a horse. His premature death posed a grave problem for the composer for it made the annual pension of 1800 florins Kinsky had assured him questionable. (National Library, Vienna)

MANUSCRIPT OF THE SONG "NEUE LIEBE, NEUES LEBEN," OPUS 75, NO. 2

This is the second of the Six Songs dedicated to Princess Kinsky. It dates from 1809 and is composed on lyrics of Goethe. (Bodmer, Zürich)

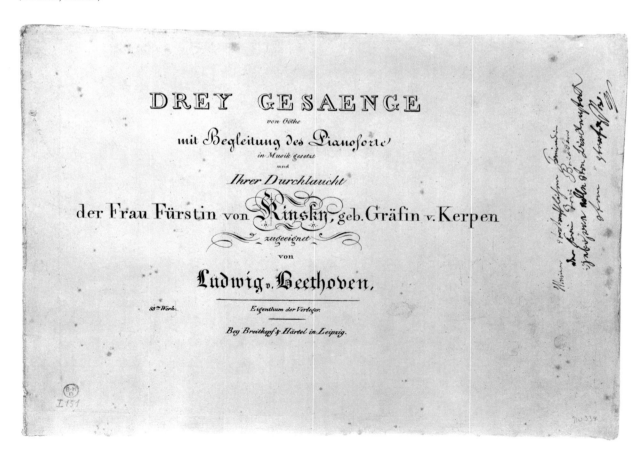

THREE GOETHE SONGS, OPUS 83

Title page with dedication to Princess Kinsky

The three songs are "Wonne der Wehmuth," "Sehnsucht," and "Mit einem gemalten Bande." They were composed in 1810 and published by Breitkopf & Härtel, Leipzig, in 1811. On the title page here reproduced Beethoven's dedication in his own handwriting: "To my excellent friend Frau Toni Brentano, née von Birkenstock." (Beethovenhaus, Bonn)

ARCHDUKE RUDOLF, BEETHOVEN DISCIPLE AND PATRON

In the winter of 1803—04, the Archduke, a passionate music lover, had become Beethoven's pupil. He studied not only piano but also composition. Despite the social disparity he became his teacher's true friend. In 1808 together with the Princes Kinsky and Lobkowitz he obligated himself to pay the composer an annuity which would keep him in Vienna.

ARCHDUKE RUDOLF OF AUSTRIA,
CARDINAL AND ARCHBISHOP OF OLMÜTZ
(1788—1831)
Oil painting
(Historical Museum of the City of Vienna)

MANUSCRIPT OF THE PIANO SONATA E FLAT MAJOR, OPUS 81 A

On the cover page of the manuscript Beethoven's words: "The Farewell—Vienna, May 4, 1809—during the departure of His Imperial Majesty—the venerable Archduke Rudolf." At the head of the first page Beethoven repeats the date: "Vienna, May 4, 1809." At the beginning of the last movement Beethoven notes: "The Arrival of His Imperial Majesty, the venerable Archduke Rudolf, January 30, 1910." The work is called the "Farewell" because it was composed on the occasion of the Archduke's absence from Vienna for several months. Written in 1809—10, it was published by Breitkopf & Härtel in Leipzig in 1811. (Society of Friends of Music, Vienna)

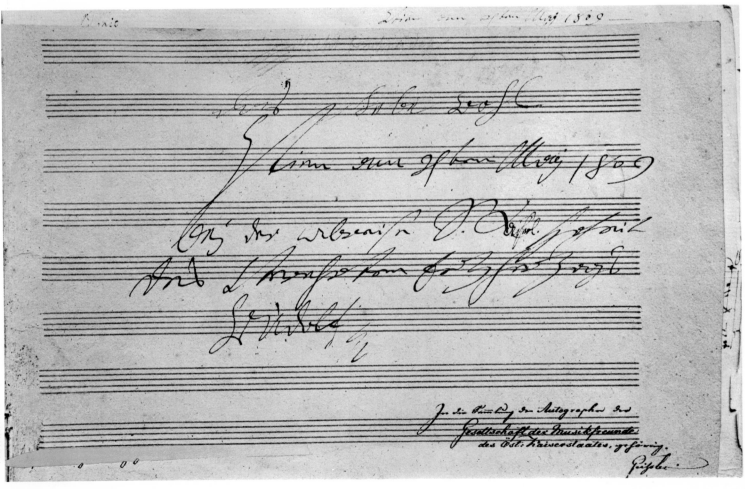

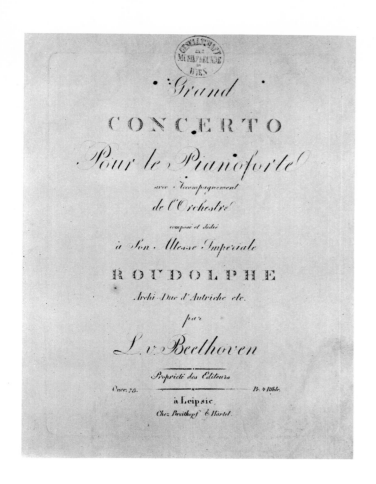

FORTY VARIATIONS ON A THEME BY BEETHOVEN,
COMPOSED BY ARCHDUKE RUDOLF
Title page with dedication to Beethoven

Most modestly the Archduke, calling his work "an assignment," identifies himself as
"by his (Beethoven's) pupil." The composition was published by Steiner in Vienna in
1819 in a collection entitled "Museum for Piano Music." (Bodmer, Zürich)

PIANO CONCERTO IN E FLAT MAJOR, No. 5, OPUS 73
Title page with dedication to Archduke Rudolf

The Concerto was completed in 1809 and published by Breitkopf & Härtel in 1811.
(Society of Friends of Music, Vienna)

AUTOGRAPH OF THE CANON FOR ARCHDUKE RUDOLF

The Canon was a New Year's greeting addressed to his Imperial disciple and patron, and bears the notation: "By your obedient servant,
L. v. Beethoven, January 1, 1820." (Society of Friends of Music, Vienna)

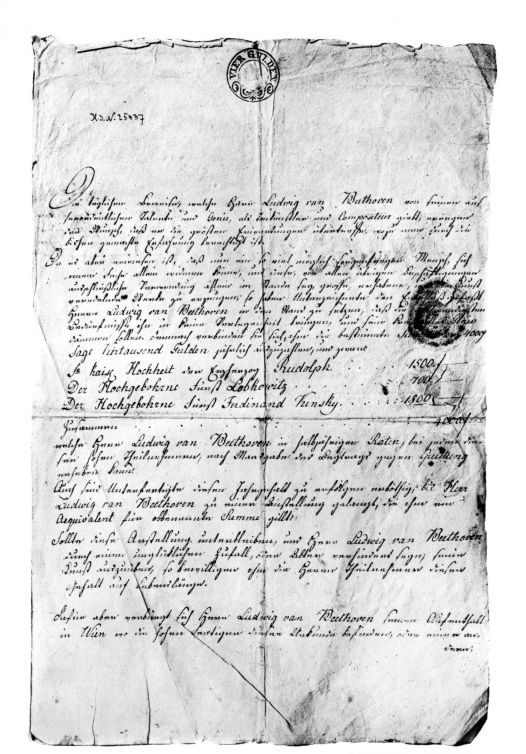

BEETHOVEN FINALLY ASSURED OF A FIXED INCOME

His financial insecurity made Beethoven attempt to obtain an annuity several times, but not before 1809 was he assured of such an income, and then through the generosity of his three patrons.

CONTRACT BETWEEN ARCHDUKE RUDOLF, PRINCE FRANZ JOSEPH MAX LOBKOWITZ AND PRINCE FERDINAND KINSKY, ON THE ONE HAND, AND LUDWIG VAN BEETHOVEN ON THE OTHER (Vienna, March 1, 1809)

Prompted by an appointment offered Beethoven by King Jérôme of Westphalia—the position of a conductor in Kassel with a fixed salary—three of his greatest admirers, the Archduke Rudolf and the Princes Kinsky and Lobkowitz, offered him an annual retainer of 4,000 florins under the condition that he would not leave Vienna. Of these 1500 florins were contributed by the Archduke, 1800 by Prince Kinsky and the balance by Prince Lobkowitz. Even though the Archduke never failed to pay his share on time, the premature death of Prince Kinsky and the devaluation of the fortune of Prince Lobkowitz were responsible for the fact that this agreement never covered the intended goal which had been to free Beethoven of financial troubles for the rest of his life. (City Library, Vienna)

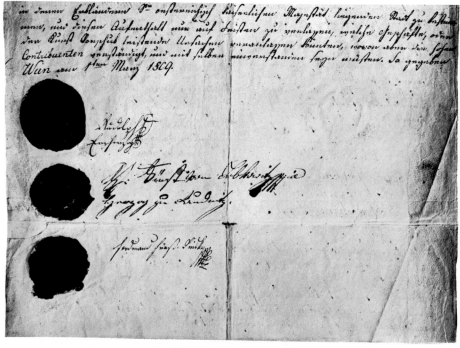

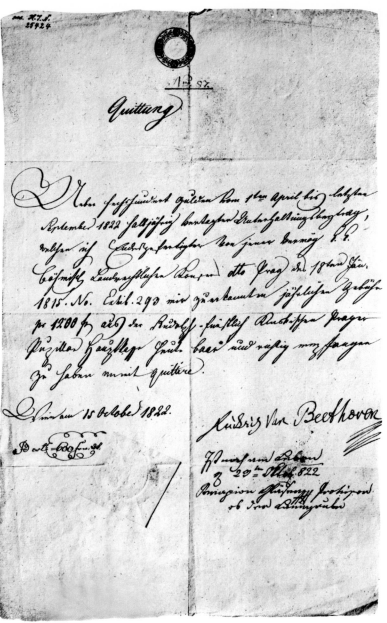

RECEIPT WITH BEETHOVEN'S SIGNATURE
(October 15, 1822)

The receipt concerns a payment of 600 gulden made by the Bank of Prince Kinsky in Prague for the months April to September, 1822. (City Library, Vienna)

RECEIPT WRITTEN BY BEETHOVEN HIMSELF
(September 1, 1814)

It acknowledges the payment of 750 gulden paid Beethoven by order of the Archduke Rudolf for the months March to August, 1814. It is entirely written in Beethoven's hand. However, Beethoven made errors and the names of the months had to be corrected. (Bodmer, Zürich)

JOHANN ANDREAS STREICHER (1761—1833)
Bronze bust by Franz Klein

Streicher, who had been Schiller's friend, married
Nanette, the daughter of a famous piano manufacturer
of Augsburg. Having entered the business of his father-
in-law, he transplanted it to Vienna where it soon
acquired considerable reputation. Streicher became an
intimate friend of Beethoven who advised him with
regard to the manufacturing of his instruments.
(Streicher Family, Vienna)

NANETTE STREICHER, NÉE STEIN (1760—1833)
Water color

A great music lover and truly talented pianist, Frau Streicher met
all the important virtuosos of Vienna in the reception rooms of the
piano firm. She made Beethoven's acquaintance, too, and beginning
in 1812 became his real guardian angel. Unselfishly and devotedly
she helped him solve his domestic problems—and these were
numerous—and she was never daunted by his financial difficulties
or the pettiness of her tasks. (Streicher Family, Vienna)

CONCERT HALL OF THE PIANO FIRM STREICHER IN VIENNA
Lithograph by F. X. Sandmann after G. Lahn

At the beginning of the nineteenth century concerts in this hall were frequent and Beethoven himself was heard here on occasion.
(Historical Museum of the City of Vienna)

PAGE FROM BEETHOVEN'S BOOK OF HOUSEHOLD ACCOUNTS
(Summer, 1825)

The page, written in ink, contains the daily expenses of the housekeeper of which he kept close track. Of Beethoven's hand are only the notes written in pencil. (Beethovenhaus, Bonn)

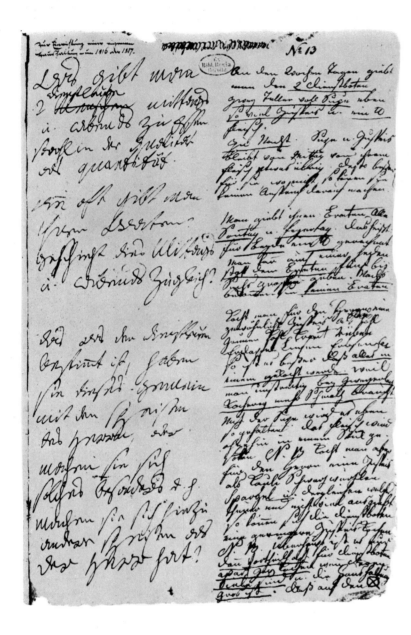

QUESTIONS PUT TO NANETTE STREICHER BY BEETHOVEN

Beethoven in 1817 asked his friend Nanette Streicher to reorganize his household which had become troublesome to him. The questions on the left side are written by Beethoven himself, the answers on the right are in Nanette's hand. (Former State Library, Berlin)

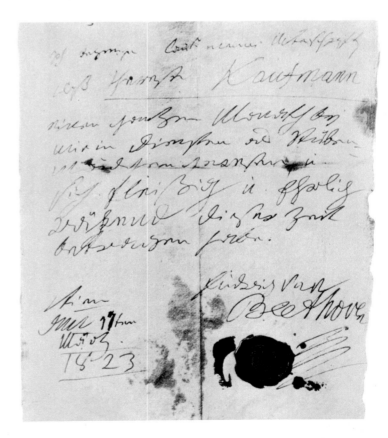

CERTIFICATE FURNISHED BY BEETHOVEN TO HIS MAID
(March 17, 1823)

This certificate for his maid Therese Kaufmann is entirely written in Beethoven's hand and testifies to his great concern with domestic problems. (Collection Figdor, Vienna)

BEETHOVEN AND THE BRENTANO FAMILY

JOHANN MELCHIOR VON BIRKENSTOCK (1738—1809)
Engraving by J. Pichler after F. H. Füger

In the hospitable home of this sensitive connoisseur much music was played and Beethoven was a frequent guest there. In 1810 he met here Bettina Brentano, Goethe's friend. (Historical Museum of the City of Vienna)

FRANZ BRENTANO (1765—1844)
Steel engraving

A native of Frankfurt, Brentano married Antonie née von Birkenstock in Vienna. Even after his return to Germany he continued to be Beethoven's benefactor and cherished his friendship. (Beethovenhaus, Bonn)

ANTONIE BRENTANO, NÉE VON BIRKENSTOCK
(1780—1869)
Engraving

To this friend "in good and in bad days" the master dedicated his Thirty-three Variations on a Waltz by Diabelli, opus 120. (Beethovenhaus, Bonn)

MAXIMILIANE VON BLITTERSDORF, NÉE BRENTANO (1802—1861)

Oil painting, unsigned

Beethoven dedicated to the daughter of the friends Franz and Antonie Brentano the Trio in One Movement and the magnificent Sonata for Piano, opus 109. (Private Collection)

AUTOGRAPH OF THE TRIO IN ONE MOVEMENT FOR PIANO, VIOLIN AND CELLO IN B FLAT MAJOR (June 2, 1812)

Beethoven composed the Trio for Maximiliane when she was but ten years old. At the head of the composition the following dedication: "For my little friend Maxe Brentano to encourage her in her piano playing." The work was published by Dunst, Frankfurt, in 1830. (Beethovenhaus, Bonn)

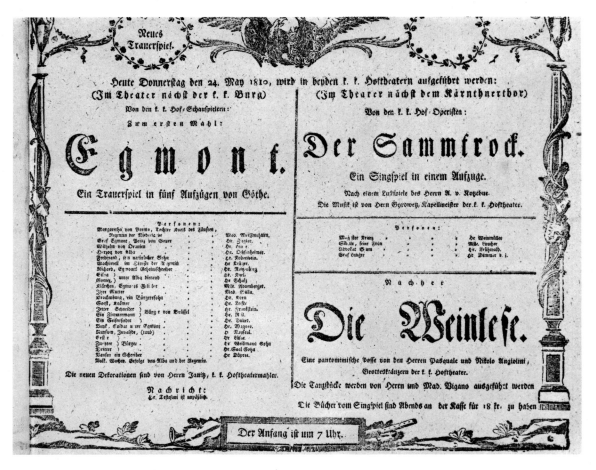

PROGRAM OF THE FIRST PERFORMANCE OF "EGMONT," A TRAGEDY BY GOETHE,
ORIGINALLY PERFORMED WITHOUT THE BEETHOVEN MUSIC

This performance took place at the Burgtheater of Vienna on the 24th of May, 1810 and had a tremendous success.
(National Library, Vienna)

THE MICHAELERPLATZ (ST. MICHAEL'S SQUARE) WITH THE OLD BURGTHEATER AT THE RIGHT
Colored engraving by Karl Postl

Here the Beethoven music to "Egmont" was heard for the first time on June 15, 1810. Later the building was
demolished. (Historical Museum of the City of Vienna)

PAGE FROM THE MANUSCRIPT OF THE "EGMONT" MUSIC, No. 4
"KLÄRCHEN'S LIED" ("FREUDVOLL UND LEIDVOLL")

The "Egmont" music of 1809—10 consists of the Overture and the four Entr'actes as well as of two Lieder sung by Klärchen and three orchestral compositions "Klärchen's Death," "Melodram" and "Victory Symphony." It is curious that Beethoven who as a rule did not approve of a simultaneous use of music and the spoken word applies just that procedure in this work, in the "Melodram." (Former State Library, Berlin)

"EGMONT UND KLÄRCHEN"
Pencil drawing by Angelica Kauffmann

This drawing was engraved by J. H. Lips and was incorporated into an illustrated edition of Goethe's works. (Goethe Museum, Weimar)

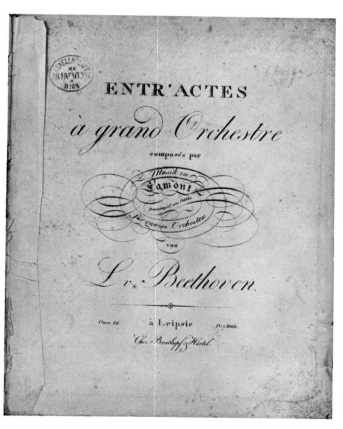

THE "EGMONT" MUSIC, OPUS 84
Title page of the first edition of the orchestral parts

The "Egmont" Overture was published in 1810 (orchestral parts only). The score of the Entr'actes music was released in 1812 by Breitkopf & Härtel, Leipzig. (Society of Friends of Music, Vienna)

141

GOETHE AND BEETHOVEN (Teplitz, July, 1812)

WOLFGANG VON GOETHE (1749—1832)
Pencil drawing by Ferdinand Jagemann, 1817

From his early youth Beethoven had felt the most sincere admiration for the greatest German poet. When he met, in 1810, Bettina von Arnim-Brentano she, also a passionate admirer of Goethe, spoke to the composer about her idol and, in turn, reported to Goethe of Beethoven's incomparable genius. Goethe, however, appreciated only the music of his friend Zelter. When the two great men met in Teplitz, Bohemia by coincidence when taking the cure, Goethe took the initiative and arranged to meet with Beethoven who was more than twenty years his junior. (Goethe Museum, Weimar)

TEPLITZ, BOHEMIA
After a colored engraving

Why did Goethe and Beethoven after their meetings on the 19th, 20th, 21st and 23rd of July, 1812 never meet again? Why did Goethe never answer Beethoven's touching letter—he was ill and in grave financial troubles—of February 8, 1823? Goethe writes on that subject to Zelter on September 2, 1812: "I met Beethoven in Teplitz. His talent is astounding; unfortunately, however, he is a completely undisciplined personality who is not entirely wrong in finding this world detestable, but who by thinking so makes that world no more pleasant for either himself or others." Such judgment coming from Goethe was identical with a complete condemnation.—Beethoven, on the other hand, declared after these meetings of Teplitz: "The atmosphere of the Court pleases Goethe too much and certainly much more than would become a poet. Let us not talk about the ridiculousness of the virtuosos if poets who should be considered the principal teachers of a nation can forget everything in view of such fallacious glamor." (Historical Museum of the City of Vienna)

BETTINA VON ARNIM, NÉE BRENTANO (1785—1859)
Pencil drawing by Ludwig Emil Grimm

Goethe's friend, particularly famous for her "Goethe's Correspondence with a Child," published the work in 1835 after the poet's death. She broke with Goethe shortly before his meeting with Beethoven in Teplitz and was compelled to leave Weimar. (Goethe Museum, Weimar)

KARL AUGUST VARNHAGEN VON ENSE (1785—1858)
Lithograph by Loeillot de Mars

Varnhagen, the husband of the famous Rahel—she, too, was one of Goethe's admirers in Weimar—revered Beethoven greatly. He had met him in Teplitz in 1811 and speaks of this meeting in his Memoirs; he also mentions him in a letter to Uhland (National Library, Vienna)

MARIANNE VON WILLEMER (1784—1860)
Pastel, 1819

At the age of sixty-five, Goethe fell madly in love with this woman who was thirty-five years his junior, and this passion inspired his immortal work "Westöstlicher Diwan," the Suleika of which is Marianne. An excellent musician, the young woman had the courage to point out to Goethe that the only composer worthy of setting his lyrics to music was Beethoven. (Goethe Museum, Weimar)

KARL FRIEDRICH ZELTER (1758—1832)
Engraving by B. H. Bendix after P. Bardon

Zelter was the director of the Berlin Singakademie and a fertile, though undoubtedly mediocre composer. As Goethe's friend he advised him on matters musical. At the outset he was unresponsive to Beethoven's genius which he did not understand. He also did not dare to acquaint Goethe with Beethoven's works until finally he, too, became an admirer of Beethoven. (Former State Library, Berlin)

CHRISTOPH AUGUST TIEDGE (1752—1841)
Engraving by Baumann and Gottschick after Weitsch

Beethoven met the poet in 1811 in Teplitz and composed his poem "An die Hoffnung." During that time Tiedge introduced Beethoven to the singer Amalie Sebald. (National Library, Vienna)

CONSTANZE ELISABETH CHARLOTTE, KNOWN AS ELISE VON DER RECKE, NÉE GRÄFIN MEDEM (1754—1833)
Engraving by E. Henne

This poetess was the friend of Tiedge and spent her vacation with him in Teplitz in 1811. She offered Beethoven her poems so he would set them to music; Beethoven did not respond at all. (National Library, Vienna)

AMALIE SEBALD
Engraving after a poem by C. Kolb

Beethoven met this eminent singer in Teplitz in 1811 and became so enamored of her that certain musicologists consider her, rather than Therese von Brunswick or Giulietta Guicciardi, the woman to whom the letter "To the Immortal Beloved" was addressed. (Society of Friends of Music, Vienna)

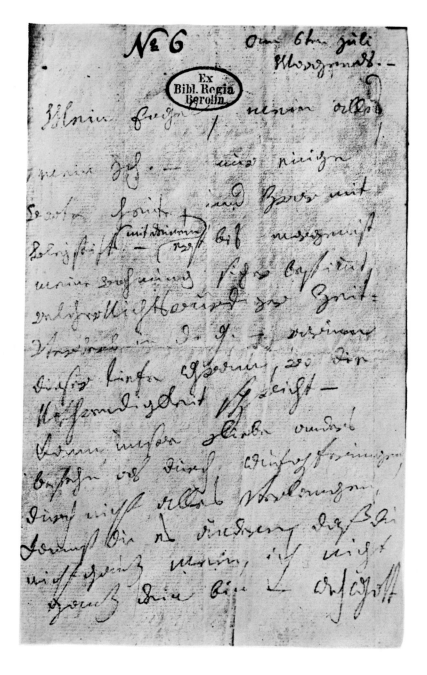

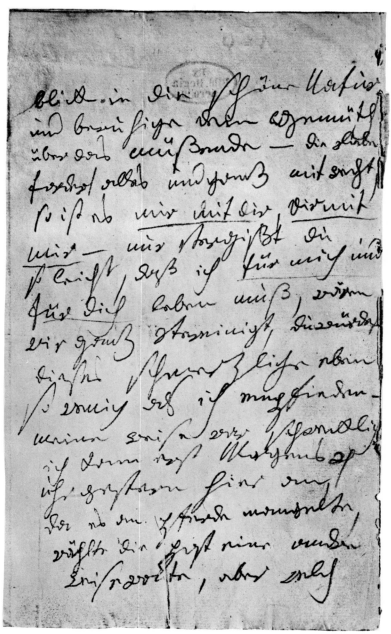

This ten page letter was found in Beethoven's desk after his death, together with the miniatures of Giulietta Guicciardi and the Countess Erdödy. The letter is dated Monday, 6th of July, and though it mentions no year it must have been written in 1812. No one knows if the letter ever reached its destination and, if it did, whether the recipient returned it to Beethoven. In its boundless style, violent and eruptive, with its exclamations and parentheses (separation marks of which, characteristic of Beethoven, finish fragments of statements), the composer cries out his passion. However, these outbursts immediately are followed by prosaic details and reasonable proposals only to resume, as abruptly, the passionate style of expression. The whole is of most astounding disorder. (Former State Library, Berlin)

DOMENICO DRAGONETTI (1763—1846)

Engraving by Bartolozzi

Beethoven met him in Vienna in 1798 and learned from him, a prodigious virtuoso on the contrabass, the particularities of this instrument. (Bibliothèque du Conservatoire, Paris)

ADALBERT GYROWETZ (1763—1850)

Engraving by J. E. Mansfeld

He was a composer of almost incredible fertility, writing pleasant works such as symphonies, chamber and church music, and also incidental music. In 1804 he became director of the orchestra of the Vienna Opera. (Society of Friends of Music, Vienna)

MUZIO CLEMENTI (1746—1832)

Engraving by A. Lemoine

The celebrated pianist and composer met Beethoven when appearing in Vienna in the spring of 1807. Beethoven was deeply impressed with Clementi's elegant playing. (Bibliothèque du Conservatoire, Paris)

MARIA-LUIGI CHERUBINI (1760—1842)

Lithograph by J. Boilly

Cherubini came to Vienna in 1805 in order to produce his opera "Lodoiska" and, in the following year, his opera "Faniska." He met Beethoven at Sonnleithner's home. Beethoven showed great enthusiasm for Cherubini's work, as had Haydn. (Public Library, Geneva)

THEODOR KÖRNER (1791—1813)
Engraving by F. X. Müller after Emma Körner

Beethoven had commissioned the young poet who died in battle at the age of twenty-three to write a libretto, yet the project failed. In the pocket of the dying soldier one found a letter by Beethoven. (Historical Museum of the City of Vienna)

JOSEPH VON HAMMER-PURGSTALL (1774—1856)
Engraving by F. John after P. Krafft

He was an Orientalist who had earned his reputation as a translator of Asiatic poetry. A great admirer of Beethoven, he introduced him to Oriental literature and suggested to him the composition of Hindu poems. (Historical Museum of the City of Vienna)

JOHANN FRIEDRICH REICHARDT (1752—1814)
Engraving by C. F. Riedel after A. Graff

The amiable composer, conductor and critic in his "Intimate Letters from Vienna," published 1808 and 1809, reports of his meetings with Beethoven. It was at his suggestion that Beethoven was offered the position of the director of the orchestra at the Court of Kassel, a position which Reichardt himself had previously occupied. (National Library, Vienna)

JOHANN FRIEDRICH ROCHLITZ (1769—1842)
Lithograph by C. Lange after A. Böhme

The director of the "Allgemeine musikalische Zeitung," a well known musicologist of his time, was one of the first to recognize the extraordinary significance of Beethoven's work and in 1822 suggested to the composer that he write a score to Goethe's "Faust." (National Library of Vienna)

GIACOMO MEYERBEER (1791—1864)
Lithograph by Delpech after Maurin

The composer in 1813 arrived in Vienna with his opera "Ali-melek" in order to win a stronghold in the Austrian capital. He met Beethoven at that time and in November 1813 played in the orchestra used in the concerts in which "The Battle of Vittoria" was heard (see page 158). (Conservatory of Music, Geneva)

LUDWIG SPOHR (1784—1859)
Engraving by J. Lier after Bodmer

This virtuoso of the violin and composer was so successful in Vienna where he arrived in 1812—in particular during a musical competition with Pierre Rode—that he was named chief conductor at the Theater an der Wien. He became acquainted with Beethoven and played the first violin in the première of the Seventh Symphony. (Collection Cortot, Lausanne)

CARL MARIA VON WEBER (1786—1826)
Lithograph by C. A. Schwerdgeburth after C. Vogel

The production of "Freischütz" in Vienna in 1822 aroused general enthusiasm and found Beethoven's particular acclaim. The following year Weber conducted "Fidelio" in Dresden and corresponded about it with Beethoven whom he later paid a visit, when he returned to Vienna in order to hear the performance of "Euryanthe." (Breitkopf & Härtel, Wiesbaden)

GIOACCHINO ANTONIO ROSSINI (1792—1868)
After a drawing by M. M. Daffinger

Rossini's "Barber of Seville" had a sensational success in Vienna in 1822. The Viennese audiences were particularly fond of Italian music. This did not make Rossini conceited and he expressly assured Beethoven of his high esteem. (Society of Friends of Music, Vienna)

Dorothea Baroness von Ertmann (1781—1849)
Miniature on ivory

This cherished friend of Beethoven was an admirable pianist and in the best sense of the word a musical artist. Beethoven recognized the genius of her interpretation in her performance of many of his works and dedicated the Piano Sonata, A major, opus 101, to her. He named the Baroness his "Dorothea-Cecilia." (Beethovenhaus, Bonn)

Greeting card of Beethoven to Baroness von Ertmann

"To the Baroness Ertmann on the New Year 1804 by her friend and admirer Beethoven." Beethoven wrote this under the vignette with two angels carrying the emblems of music—one the golden lyre, the other the pencil ready to record inspiration. (Bodmer, Zürich)

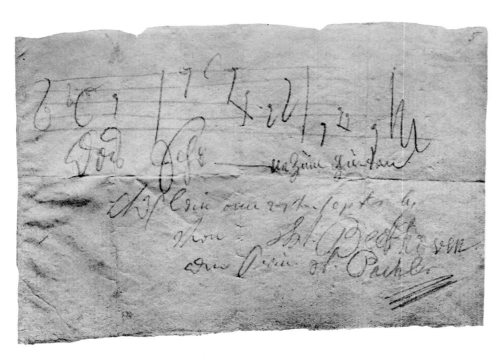

Album page with Beethoven's writing to Marie Pachler-Koschak

Beethoven wrote to his friend Marie Pachler three measures and the words: "The beautiful to the good. Vösslau, 27 September, (1823) by Ludwig van Beethoven for Frau von Pachler." (Society of Friends of Music, Vienna)

Marie Leopoldine Pachler-Koschak (1794—1855)
Miniature on ivory

The composer met this excellent pianist in Vienna in 1817 and wrote about her: "Never before have I found anyone who interprets my compositions as well as she does, and I do not except the great pianists who have only technique or affectations. (Society of Friends of Music, Vienna)

BEETHOVEN

Cast by Franz Klein in 1812

Klein had received the commission for a bust of Beethoven by Streicher, the manufacturer of pianos, and was given permission (probably not without difficulties) to make a plaster cast of his face. This mask is therefore absolutely authentic and allows us to study Beethoven's facial characteristics exactly. The composer was forty-two years old. Most of the later portraits were inspired by this mask. (Beethovenhaus, Bonn)

BEETHOVEN

Bronze bust by Franz Klein

It was created after the cast. (Streicher, Krumpendorf)

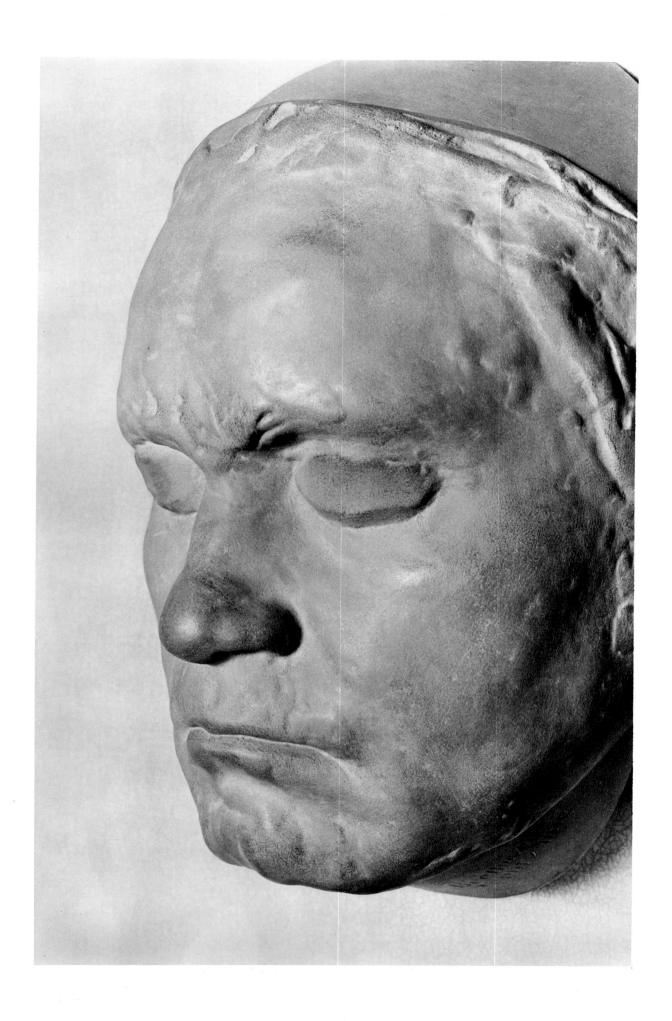

SEVENTH SYMPHONY,
A MAJOR, OPUS 92

*A page from the autograph
showing measures 72 to 80 of
the Allegretto*

The composition was begun in
the fall of 1811 and completed
in June, 1812. It was dedicated
to his patron Count Moritz von
Fries. The first performance
took place December 8, 1813 in
the Hall of the University of
Vienna. The manuscript of the
Symphony is, at this time, missing. (Former State Library,
Berlin)

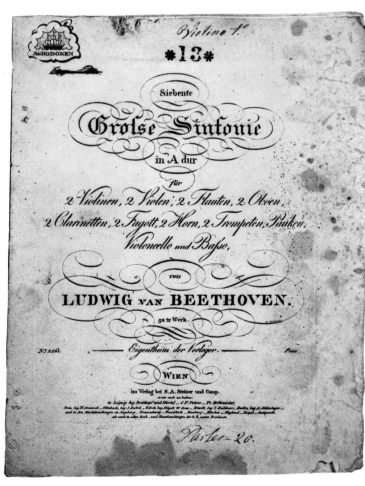

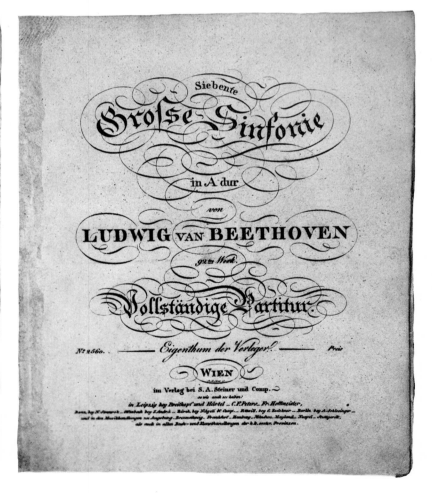

THE FIRST EDITIONS OF THE SEVENTH SYMPHONY

Orchestral parts, title page
(van Hoboken, Ascona)

Score, title page
(Society of Friends of Music, Vienna)

The various editions (orchestral parts, score and various transcriptions) were published by Steiner & Cie, Vienna, in 1816. The dedication to von Fries can be found in the inside of these editions.

First page of the first movement

The Symphony was completed October, 1812 in Linz and was
premiered, together with other works of the master, at the
Grosse Redoutensaal (Masquerade Hall), in Vienna on February
27, 1814. (Former State Library, Berlin)

FIRST EDITIONS OF THE EIGHTH SYMPHONY

The title pages of the *orchestral parts* and the *score*

Steiner & Cie published—similarly to the Seventh Symphony—
seven different editions of the Eighth Symphony in 1817. (van
Hoboken, Ascona; Society of Friends of Music, Vienna)

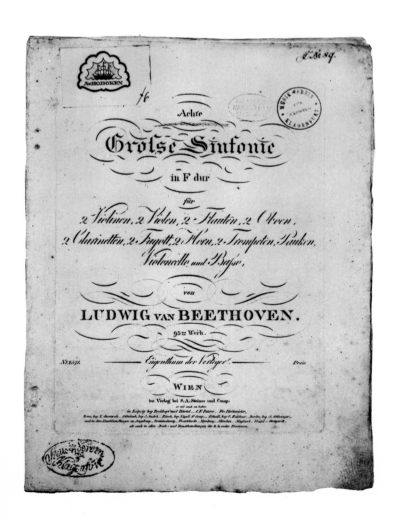

AUGUST VON KOTZEBUE (1761—1819)

Engraving by J. F. Bolt

Beethoven made the poet's acquaintance in 1803, accepted his proposal to write a prelude and postlude for the Inaugural Festival of the Opera in Budapest. The Prelude was called "King Stephan, Hungary's First Benefactor," and the Postlude "The Ruins of Athens." Both scores were written within a few weeks, in 1811, and the opening of the new Opera was on February 9, 1812. (Historical Museum of the City of Vienna)

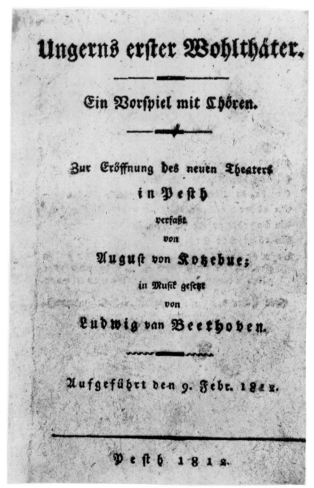

LIBRETTO OF "HUNGARY'S FIRST BENEFACTOR"

Beethoven's music, opus 117, consists of an Overture, five Choruses, a Victory March, two Melodrams and a final Chorus. (City Library, Vienna)

LIBRETTO TO "THE RUINS OF ATHENS"

Beethoven's music, opus 113, consists of an Overture, five Choruses, several Arias and two Marches. (City Library, Vienna)

MASKED BALL IN THE GROSSE REDOUTENSAAL OF THE HOFBURG

Water color by Joseph Schütz

Masked balls, theatrical productions, concerts and a thousand other social events scheduled for the duration of the Congress of Vienna lent it the atmosphere of permanent festivity. In the above hall where works of Beethoven had been performed previously the much quoted concert of November 29, 1814 took place under the direction of the composer. (Historical Museum of the City of Vienna)

A SESSION OF THE CONGRESS

Engraving by J. Godefrey after J. B. Isabey

This well known picture of the painter Isabey shows the representatives of the various countries participating in the Congress. At the right, at the end of the table, we see Prince Talleyrand-Périgord representing France. He tried to save whatever possible, after Napoleon's disaster, for his country. Vis-à-vis is Prince Metternich, the Austrian Chancellor, who introduces the representative of England, the Duke of Wellington, to the conference. (Historical Museum of the City of Vienna)

ANNOUNCEMENT OF THE CONCERT

For the monarchs convened in Vienna with their entourages, Beethoven conducted an "Akademie" devoted entirely to the performance of his own works. The program consisted of the Seventh Symphony, the cantata "The Glorious Moment," then a "war symphony" in honor of the great Admiral Wellington entitled "Wellington's Victory." Despite the undeniable deficiencies of the latter work the audience, elegant and enthusiastic, made this concert the zenith of Beethoven's career. (Beethovenhaus, Bonn)

"WELLINGTON'S VICTORY OR THE BATTLE OF VITTORIA," OPUS 91

Title page of the piano score transcribed by Beethoven himself

When on July 27, 1813 the news of Wellington's victory reached Vienna, Beethoven, impressed, immediately set to work on this warlike music and dedicated it to George IV of England. The mediocre work was published in 1816 by Steiner & Cie in Vienna. (Bodmer, Zürich)

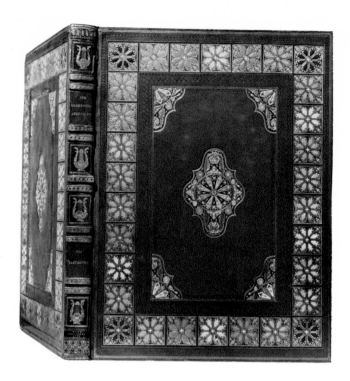

"THE GLORIOUS MOMENT," CANTATA FOR SOLI, CHORUS AND ORCHESTRA, OPUS 136

Cover   *Title page*

The Cantata, on a text by Aloys Weissenbach, was written in the fall of 1814 on the occasion of the Congress of Vienna. It was first performed on November 29 of that year, and in 1835 was published in a de luxe edition of just a few copies. Three were for the persons to whom the work was dedicated: Franz I, Emperor of Austria; Nicolas I, Czar of Russia, and Friedrich Wilhelm III, King of Prussia. The publisher Haslinger kept several other copies for himself and later offered them at 200 florins per copy. A more modest edition was readied for subscription in 1837 at 15 florins. The copy here reproduced was presented to the Czar. (Bodmer, Zürich)

FRANZ WILD (1792—1860)   ANNA MILDER-HAUPTMANN   ANTON FORTI (1790—1859)
Engraving by F. John after Létronne   (1785—1838)   Lithograph by J. Lanzedelly
                                   Engraving by Leybold

These singers were the stars of the Vienna Opera and participated in the first performance of the cantata "The Glorious Moment." (National Library, Vienna)

159

SIGMUND ANTON STEINER (1773—1838)
Lithograph by J. Kriehuber

TOBIAS HASLINGER (1787—1842)
Lithograph by J. Teltscher

In 1803 Steiner had taken over the old printing plant of Senefelder and conducted the business as Steiner & Cie. Haslinger entered the business in 1810, became a partner in 1814 and sole proprietor in 1826, then giving the house his own name. Beethoven's relationship to the publishing house dates from 1814. In his numerous letters to the owners Steiner and Haslinger he jokingly calls the former Lieutenant General, the latter the young adjutant, and himself—"Generalissimus." (National Library, Vienna)

THE INTERIOR OF THE HASLINGER MUSIC STORE IN VIENNA
Water color by Franz Weigl

Beethoven established most cordial relations with both Steiner and Haslinger and paid them frequent visits in their store at the Paternostergässchen near St. Stephan's Cathedral. After a renovation of the store he wrote his publishers: "Good luck in your newly painted place of business. Now be sure that your nest becomes a beer place because beer drinkers are good musicians and one should see them at your place. Yours most devoted Beethoven." (Haslinger Archive, Vienna)

HOUSE IN WHICH BEETHOVEN LIVED:
MÖLKERBASTEI, VIENNA

After an engraving by L. Grüner

Beethoven lived here for the first time in 1804. It afforded him
a broad view of the countryside. The building was owned by
Baron Pasqualati, a rich merchant and music lover. The irascible
composer several times gave up the apartment, frequently under
unessential pretexts. However, he always seemed happy when
returning to the hospitable home.

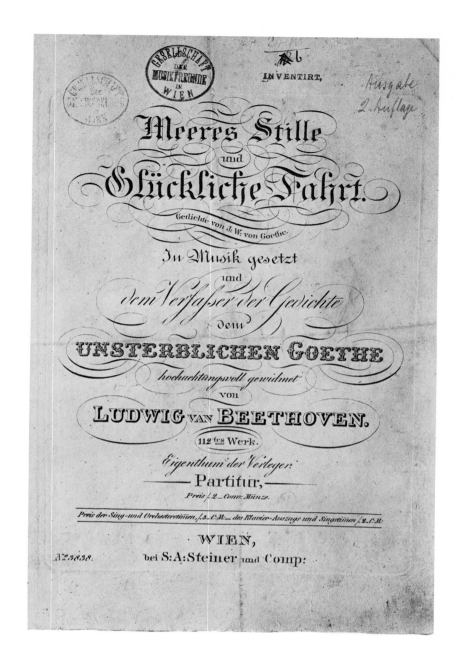

"CALM SEA AND PROSPEROUS VOYAGE"
POETRY BY GOETHE SET FOR SOPRANO,
ALTO, TENOR AND BASS WITH ORCHESTRAL
ACCOMPANIMENT, OPUS 112

Title page with dedication to "the author of these poems,
the immortal Goethe."

Completed in 1815, published in 1822 by Steiner & Cie in
Vienna. The first performance took place on December 25,
1815. (Society of Friends of Music, Vienna)

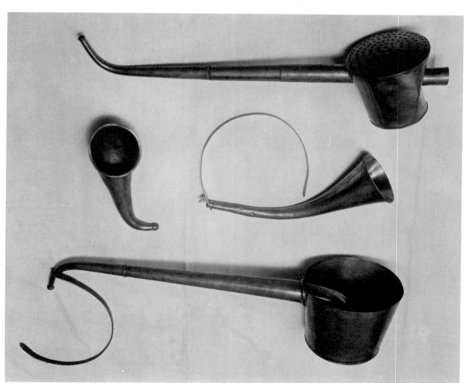

HEARING AIDS CONSTRUCTED FOR BEETHOVEN
BETWEEN 1812 AND 1814 BY MÄLZEL,
THE INVENTOR OF THE METRONOME

Because of his growing deafness Beethoven had ordered
these instruments which really were of little help to him.
Nevertheless he always had the smallest one close by for
ready use. (Beethovenhaus, Bonn)

LUDWIG VAN BEETHOVEN

Pencil drawing by Gustav Adolph Hippius

There are doubts as to the date of this portrait. Hippius was in Vienna between early 1814 and 1816, and it is assumed that the drawing dates from 1815. (Bodmer, Zürich)

LUDWIG VAN BEETHOVEN

Oil portrait by Christoph Heckel

This portrait is thought to have been created in 1815 in the music salon of the piano manufacturer Streicher in Vienna. (Collection Lichtenberger, Heidelberg)

LUDWIG VAN BEETHOVEN

Lithograph by A. Hatzfeld after a different portrait of Beethoven by C. Heckel

The portrait, made shortly after the previous one, dates from either 1815 or 1816. (Beethovenhaus, Bonn)

Ludwig van Beethoven (1815)

Oil painting by Willibord Joseph Mähler

This is the second of four Beethoven portraits by Mähler and was commissioned by Baron Ignaz von Gleichenstein, Beethoven's friend. (Gleichenstein Collection)

Ludwig van Beethoven (1815)

Oil painting by Willibord Joseph Mähler

This is the third painting of Mähler, part of the painter's estate. (Collection Karajan, Salzburg)

Ludwig van Beethoven (1815)

Oil painting by Willibord Joseph Mähler

This, the fourth and last portrait by the painter, after his death passed into the hands of Joseph von Sonnleithner, and afterwards became the property of its present owner. (Society of Friends of Music, Vienna)

LUDWIG VAN BEETHOVEN (1814)
Engraving by Blasius Höfel after Létronne

The engraver Höfel found the original portrait of Létronne to be wanting in fidelity. In order to give the portrait the highest degree of similitude he obtained Beethoven's permission to do a new portrait for which Beethoven consented to sit. The result was so convincing that the friends of the master agreed that the engraving was "of extreme likeness." Beethoven himself, too, was well pleased with the work which he gave to several of his friends as presents. (Society of Friends of Music, Vienna)

RAHEL VARNHAGEN VON ENSE
NÉE ROBERT-LEVIN (1771—1833)
Pastel by M. M. Daffinger

Beethoven met Rahel, this extraordinary woman, for the first time in Teplitz in 1811. At that time Rahel—she was forty—had had several romances. With her charm and her intellect she knew how to win Beethoven's heart quickly. According to Kaznelson and his recent book, Beethoven is supposed to have written the song cycle "To the Distant Beloved" for her.

"TO THE DISTANT BELOVED," SONG CYCLE BY ALOYS JEITTELES, SET FOR VOICE AND PIANO BY BEETHOVEN, OPUS 98

Title page with dedication to Prince Lobkowitz

This succession of lieder was composed in 1816 and in that year appeared under the imprint of Steiner & Cie, Vienna. (Society of Friends of Music, Vienna)

164

AUTOGRAPH OF THE LIEDER "TO THE DISTANT BELOVED," OPUS 98

On this title page in Beethoven's hand: "To the Distant Beloved, six Lieder by Aloys Jeitteles, set to music by L. v. Beethoven."
(Beethoven Archive, Bonn)

FIRST PAGE OF THE AUTOGRAPH OF THE SONG CYCLE

At the beginning of the first Lied Beethoven noted: "Rather slow and with expression—1816 in the month of April."
(Beethoven Archive, Bonn)

BEETHOVEN IN BADEN NEAR VIENNA

In the years 1807, 1810, 1813, 1814 and 1817 during the summers Beethoven stayed in Baden near Vienna to take the cure. In 1815 and 1816 he stayed there for quite some time. Later, from 1821 to 1825, he again returned to Baden to take the waters.

BADEN NEAR VIENNA, THE THERMAL SPRINGS
Colored engraving by Vincenz Grüner after V. Grimm
(Historical Museum of the City of Vienna)

THE HELENA VALLEY NEAR BADEN
After a water color

Beethoven, who was an inveterate walker, showed particular affection for this beautiful valley.
(Historical Museum of the City of Vienna)

THE CHURCH OF HEILIGENSTADT
Crayon with sepia by A. Hofmann

Beethoven stayed in Heiligenstadt from the middle of May to the end of June, 1817. Then he returned for some time to Vienna and from there went to Nussdorf where he remained the rest of the summer. (Beethovenhaus, Bonn)

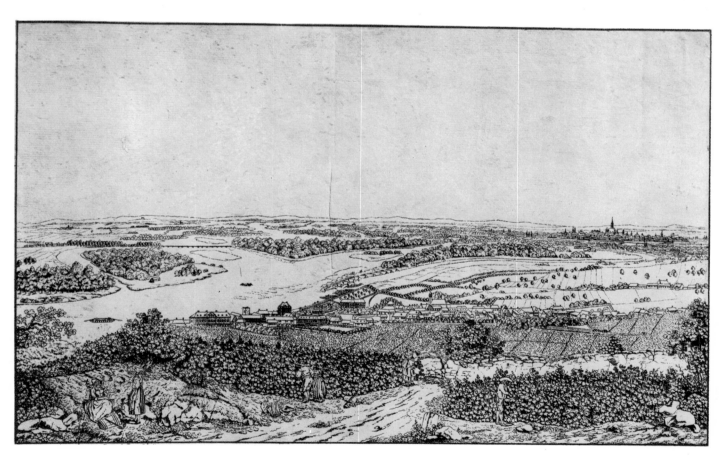

NUSSDORF WITH VIENNA IN THE BACKGROUND
Colored engraving by Joseph and Peter Schaffer

Always enamored of country life, Beethoven in July, 1817 elected the little hamlet of Nussdorf for his summer vacation and later returned several times. (Historical Museum of the City of Vienna)

MÖDLING NEAR VIENNA
Colored engraving, unsigned

Beethoven had made the acquaintance of this charming place in 1799, but it was not until the summers of 1818 through 1821 that he made frequent journeys there. Here he took long walks and lived for his relaxation and recreation. In Mödling Beethoven worked on the composition of opus 106, the piano sonata, on the Missa Solemnis and on the Ninth Symphony. (Historical Museum of the City of Vienna)

THE COURTYARD OF THE POTTER JAKOB TUSCHECK IN MÖDLING

Beethoven spent the summers of 1818 and 1819 in this old house; during his second stay there he worked particularly on the Credo of the Missa Solemnis. (Historical Museum of the City of Vienna)

Letter of Beethoven to Archduke Rudolf of Austria (1819)

Fragment

On the third line of the page herewith reproduced Beethoven wrote: "The day when a solemn Mass of my composition is executed—on the occasion of festivities that are organized in the honor of your Imperial Majesty—will be the most beautiful day of my life, and I pray that God will inspire me so that my feeble efforts can contribute to the glory of that festive day." Beethoven made reference to his composition of the Missa Solemnis in honor of his great patron who on March 19, 1820, had become Cardinal of Olmütz. (Society of Friends of Music, Vienna)

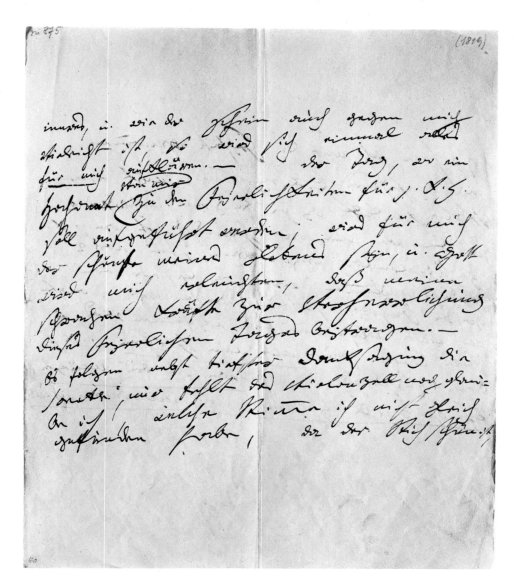

Page from a Sketchbook of Ludwig van Beethoven

In this sketchbook there are numerous notes on the "Variations on a Waltz by Diabelli" and a great many comments on the Missa Solemnis. Indeed, particularly with reference to the latter and to the origin of the work which Beethoven himself considered his chief composition this sketchbook is of compelling interest. (Bodmer, Zürich)

Portrait, charcoal with chalk, by August Karl Friedrich von Klöber

The painter Klöber, due to the mediation of the cellist Jakob Dont in 1818 when Beethoven was in Mödling, received permission to do a portrait of the composer and his nephew Karl. He painted both in life-size, choosing as a background the scene of Brühl near Mödling. Unfortunately the painting has disappeared. The drawing reproduced here dates also from 1818 and probably is a study which later led to the double portrait. (C. F. Peters, Leipzig)

Beethoven's hands

Crayon drawing by A. von Klöber

This, too, is a sketch preceding the double portrait. (Bodmer, Zürich)

LUDWIG VAN BEETHOVEN

Crayon portrait by A. von Klöber

This is another sketch for the large double portrait by Klöber. (Bodmer, Zürich)

LUDWIG VAN BEETHOVEN

Oil painting after Ferdinand Schimon

During the years 1818 and 1819 in which Beethoven worked on the Missa Solemnis, Ferdinand Schimon, a young painter and singer, tried to obtain the composer's permission for the portrait. Beethoven refused the request until Schindler intervened. Finally Schimon was permitted to put his easel into the composer's studio so that he could gradually and quietly work on the portrait. However, the eyes of the master were never completed. — Suddenly changing his decision Beethoven then invited Schimon a number of times to have coffee with him so the painter would have the opportunity to complete the portrait during the leisure hours of the composer. The first owner of the portrait was Schindler, but later it came into the possession of the State Library in Berlin. (Beethovenhaus, Bonn)

LUDWIG VAN BEETHOVEN

Oil portrait by Josef Karl Stieler

Beethoven conceded Stieler three sittings only for this portrait, which dates from 1819. As a result the painter was not given a chance to complete the work. This undoubtedly is also the reason why the hands in this portrait essentially differ from those in other Beethoven portraits. — The inscription "Missa Solemnis" which one can read on the score held by the composer was probably put there at Beethoven's special request for he was at that time in the midst of working on that composition. (C. F. Peters, Leipzig)

FRANZ SCHUBERT (1797—1828)
Oil portrait by Wilhelm August Rieder

Even though Beethoven and Schubert lived in the same city and each had his circle of friends (they even had some admirers in common) Beethoven made Schubert's acquaintance—curiously enough—only when the latter brought him his "Variations for Piano for four hands," opus 10. In 1822 Schubert dedicated this work to Beethoven. Even though Beethoven held his young colleague in high esteem there was nevertheless no close relationship between them. (Schubert Museum, Vienna)

VARIATIONS ON A FRENCH CHANSON
FOR PIANO, FOUR HANDS, OPUS 10
BY FRANZ SCHUBERT

The work was composed in 1821 and published at Cappi and Diabelli in Vienna the following year. Schubert dedicated it to the master more than twice his age—Schubert was only twenty-four. (Society of Friends of Music, Vienna)

ANTON SCHINDLER (1795—1864)

After a photograph

Schindler was born in Meidel, Moravia and had come to Vienna to study law without, however, renouncing the serious study of the violin. He soon succeeded in obtaining a position with the orchestra of the Theater an der Wien which, for a time, he conducted. Through this position he made Beethoven's acquaintance and developed a glowing enthusiasm for Beethoven's œuvre. In 1819 he became an associate in the office of the attorney Bach who was Beethoven's lawyer. His contact with Beethoven became so steady that hardly a day passed without their speaking to one another. Finally, Schindler became Beethoven's indispensable companion.

The famous "Conversation books" through which Beethoven notwithstanding his increasing deafness could continue to speak to his friends prove Schindler's devotion and patience. Moreover, they reflect the self-denial with which Schindler accepted many unfair reproaches of the easily irritated master without contradiction. It is only fair to add, however, that Beethoven, once he had recognized his injustice, hastened to repair the aggravation he had caused, by the most touching manifestations of friendship. However, this did not prevent him from sacrificing Schindler—during the years 1825 and 1826—as a result of imagined injustice received from him. It was at that time that the violinist Karl Holz, who had succeeded in gaining Beethoven's confidence, took Schindler's place. Far from bearing a grudge as a result of Beethoven's insults, Schindler took his place again as soon as Beethoven needed him, and in the most touching manner took care of the master during the latter's last and most terrible illness. After Beethoven's death he worked for many years on a book that he wished to create as a monument to the revered genius. Not until 1840 did he publish his Beethoven biography, the work which despite several errors became the basis of all Beethoven biographies. (Beethovenhaus, Bonn)

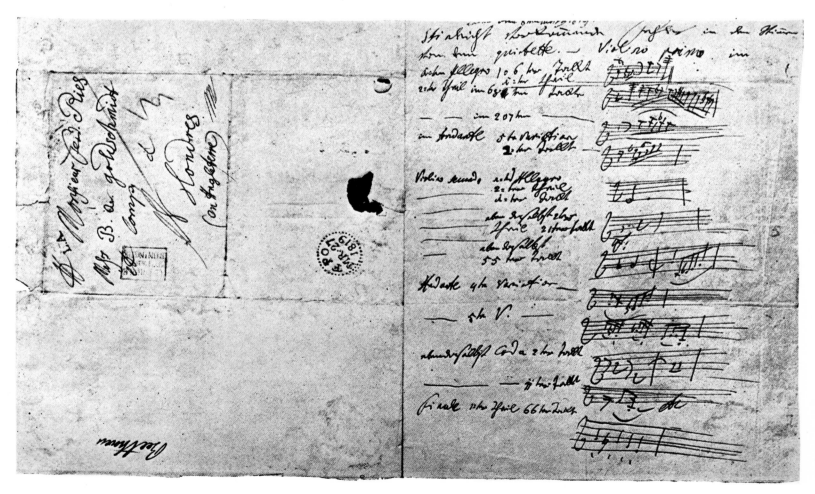

BEETHOVEN'S LETTER TO FERDINAND RIES (March 8, 1819)

Beethoven wrote this letter to his old pupil Ries, who was then living in London, on the subject of one of his quintets which was to be published by an English publisher: "Vienna, March 8, 1819. This pertains to possible errors which could appear in the parts of the Quintet . . ." There follow three pages of corrections which he asked Ries to communicate to the publisher. (Collection Wegeler, Koblenz)

LUDWIG VAN BEETHOVEN
Marble bust by Anton Dietrich

On the right side of the socle the inscription "Anton Dietrich modelled after the life, 1821." (Historical Museum of the City of Vienna)

LUDWIG VAN BEETHOVEN
Lithograph by Faust Herr after Anton Dietrich

This Beethoven portrait dates from the same time in which the two busts were made. (National Library, Vienna)

LUDWIG VAN BEETHOVEN
Ivory bust by Anton Dietrich

This second Beethoven bust, created by the Viennese sculptor Dietrich, dates from 1822. (National Gallery, Berlin)

OPENING OF THE THEATER IN THE JOSEFSTADT, VIENNA (1822)

ANNOUNCEMENT OF THE OPENING OF THE THEATER, OCTOBER 3, 1822

The memorable evening was opened by Beethoven's Overture "The Consecration of the House," opus 124, and by a Prologue of the dramaturgist Carl Meisl. (City Library, Vienna)

INTERIOR OF THE THEATER IN THE JOSEFSTADT, VIENNA
Colored engraving

(Historical Museum of the City of Vienna)

ANNOUNCEMENT OF THE REVIVAL OF "FIDELIO," NOVEMBER 3, 1822

This revival of the opera had an extraordinary success due to no small degree to the eminent singer Wilhelmine Schröder-Devrient, then a guest artist in Vienna. (National Library, Vienna)

WILHELMINE SCHRÖDER-DEVRIENT (1804—1860)

Lithograph by W. Santer

The incomparable singer and actress in the role of Leonore. (National Library, Vienna)

ANTON HAIZINGER (1796—1869)

Portrait unsigned

Haizinger was the magnificent Florestan of 1822. (Historical Museum of the City of Vienna)

"Fidelio"
A set of frescoes by Moritz von Schwind

Schwind, the famous painter, created a series of frescoes with scenes from "Fidelio" for the Vienna Opera. On this page, three are reproduced.

Act I, Scene IV

Act II, Scene III

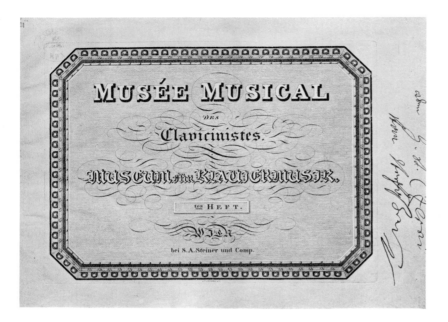

PIANO SONATA IN A MAJOR, OPUS 101

Title page with Beethoven's autograph dedication to Carl Czerny

The Sonata was completed in 1816 and published in 1817 by Steiner & Cie in Vienna. It was part of a collection called "Musée musical des Clavicinistes." Beethoven dedicated the work to Baroness Dorothea Ertmann. (Society of Friends of Music, Vienna)

THE "HAMMERKLAVIER SONATA" IN B FLAT MAJOR, OPUS 106

Title page with the dedication to Archduke Rudolf of Austria

The work, partly composed in Mödling during the summer of 1818, was published by Artaria & Cie in Vienna in September, 1819. (Society of Friends of Music, Vienna)

THE E MAJOR PIANO SONATA, OPUS 109

Title page with dedication to Maximiliane Brentano

This work was dedicated to the daughter of his friends Franz and Antonie Brentano. Composed in 1820, it was published the following year simultaneously by Schlesinger in Berlin and by Artaria, Cappi & Diabelli, and Steiner in Vienna. (Society of Friends of Music, Vienna)

THE PIANO SONATA IN A FLAT MAJOR, OPUS 110

Title page

This, one of the main works of the piano literature, was completed on December 25, 1821 and was published in July, 1822 simultaneously in Paris, Berlin, Vienna and London. (van Hoboken, Ascona)

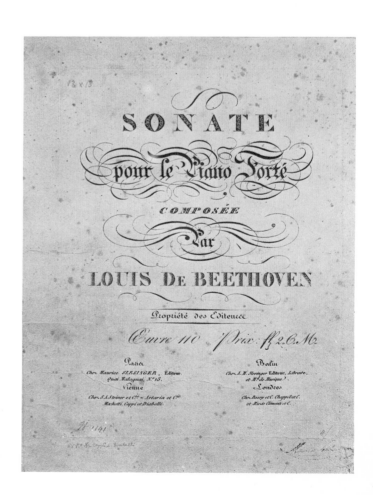

Autograph of the Piano Sonata in C minor, opus 111

First page of the first movement

On the upper left corner of the first page Beethoven's pencilled notation "January 13, 1822"; however, the note is now hardly legible. The annotation at the bottom of the page was made by the publisher Artaria who owned the manuscript. On the right margin a note in Beethoven's hand. This is a precious autograph, a copy of which exists in the Former State Library in Berlin, which in 1903 became part of the collection of the Beethoven Archive in Bonn.

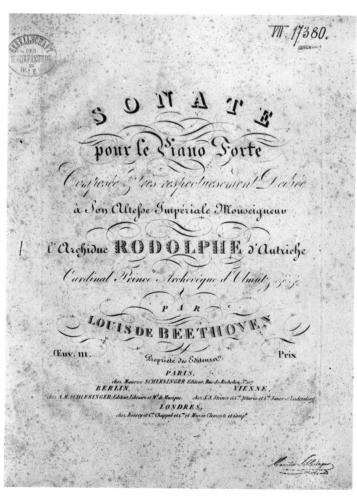

Piano Sonata in C minor, opus 111

Title page with dedication to Archduke Rudolf of Austria

This last of Beethoven's piano sonatas was first published, in April, 1823, by Schlesinger in Paris. Since the engraved copy contained many errors Schlesinger prepared a new edition in Berlin. (Society of Friends of Music, Vienna)

KARL HOLZ (1798—1858)

Ivory miniature by Barbara Fröhlich

Holz was the violinist in the Schuppanzigh Quartet. He met Beethoven and gained his confidence. In 1826 he replaced the faithful Schindler and Beethoven commissioned him with the writing of his biography. Only during Beethoven's last illness did Schindler take his old place as Beethoven's closest friend. (Historical Museum of the City of Vienna)

ANTON DIABELLI (1781—1858)

Lithograph by Josef Kriehuber

Having arrived in Vienna in 1804, Diabelli was originally a teacher of piano and guitar. He later became an associate of the publisher Cappi and finally published music under his own name beginning 1824. Besides, Diabelli was a fertile composer. Beethoven, referring to Diabelli's publishing activities, often gave him the nickname "diabolus." (National Library, Vienna)

33 VARIATIONS FOR PIANO ON A WALTZ BY DIABELLI, OPUS 120,
BY LUDWIG VAN BEETHOVEN

In 1819 the publisher and composer Diabelli requested a number of composers who had won reputation to write variations on a waltz he had composed himself. Among those asked were, in addition to Beethoven, Schubert and Liszt. Beethoven, not averse to the idea, wrote, instead of the one variation, thirty-three. They form his opus 120 and were published, as a separate publication, by Cappi & Diabelli in 1823. This didactic composition was dedicated to his friend Antonie Brentano, née Birkenstock. (Society of Friends of Music, Vienna)

DIPLOMA CERTIFYING THE HONORARY CITIZENSHIP
OF BEETHOVEN AS CONFERRED UPON HIM
BY THE MUNICIPALITY OF VIENNA

On November 16, 1815 the city of Vienna, wishing to distinguish the composer for his exceptional merits and to bind him further to the residence of his choice, made him an honorary citizen. (City Library, Vienna)

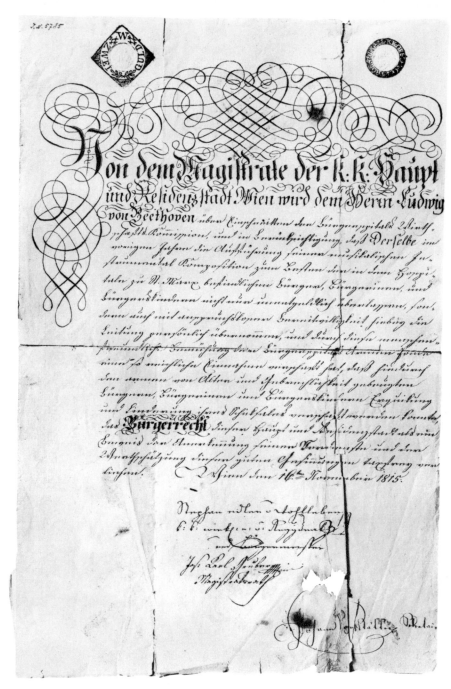

DIPLOMA OF MEMBERSHIP
IN THE ROYAL MUSIC ACADEMY OF STOCKHOLM

On December 28, 1822 the Music Academy of Stockholm honored itself by making Beethoven one of its members. A similar distinction was conferred upon him by the Academy of Amsterdam. (Former State Library, Berlin)

THE PROJECT OF THE COMPLETE EDITION OF BEETHOVEN'S WORKS

The publishers Steiner and Haslinger harbored the plan of a complete edition of Beethoven's works for a long time. They had the first works of the master copied on large folio pages at great expense. After one or two works had been engraved the publishers suddenly were terrified by the magnitude of the task and decided to discontinue the enterprise. The already completed copies were bought by Archduke Rudolf but with the condition that the remainder of Beethoven's entire work would be copied on such folio pages. This total work fills more than thirty large volumes and today is owned by the Society of Friends of Music, Vienna.

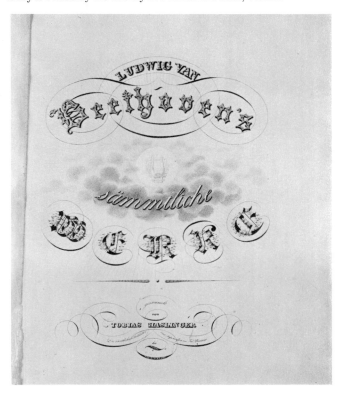

TITLE PAGE OF THE COMPLETE EDITION,
MANUSCRIPT

ONE OF THE FIRST PAGES OF THE COMPLETE EDITION,
MANUSCRIPT
The Beethoven signature is of his own hand

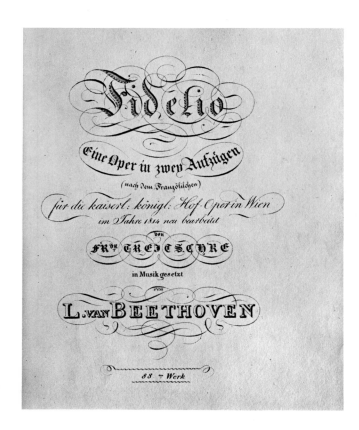

TITLE PAGE OF "FIDELIO"
OF THE COMPLETE EDITION, MANUSCRIPT

FIRST PAGE OF THE STRING QUARTET IN E FLAT MAJOR,
OPUS 74, OF THE COMPLETE EDITION, MANUSCRIPT

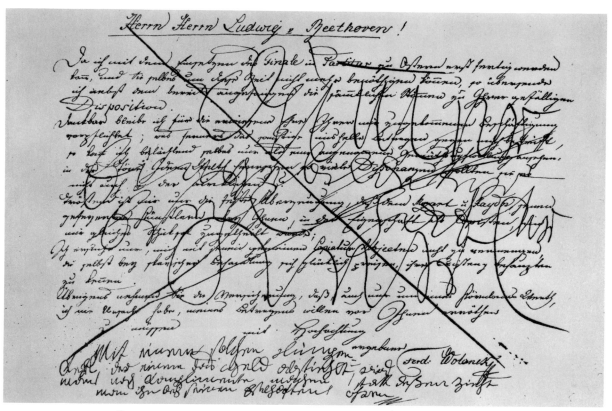

LETTER OF THE COPYIST WOLANEK TO BEETHOVEN (without date)

Wolanek was tired of the thankless job of putting into clear writing Beethoven's frequently illegible manuscripts. He wrote him this letter in which he reminded the composer of the work he had done for Mozart and Haydn, and in which he made some observations with regard to Beethoven and the voluntary termination of services. When Beethoven received the letter he was beside himself and furiously struck out the entire text, and in mammoth letters wrote "a stupid pretentious and asinine person." Then, at the bottom of the page, he remarked "one should pay no compliments to such an individual who only steals one's money, one should just pull his ass's ears." (Beethovenhaus, Bonn)

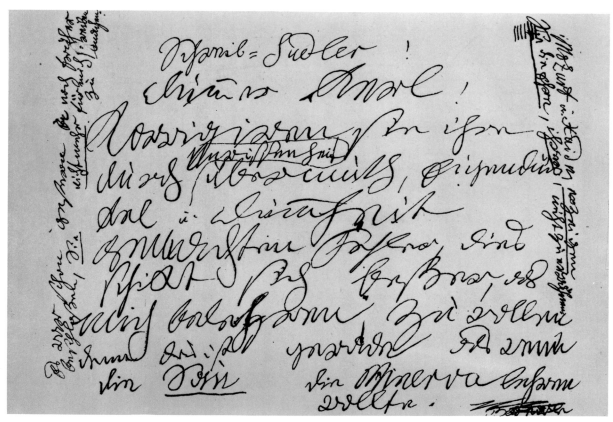

BACKPAGE OF THE SAME LETTER WITH BEETHOVEN'S REPLY

"You scratcher, you idiot! You had better correct your mistakes which are the results of your ignorance, your arrogance, your conceit and your stupidity. That would be better than trying to teach me. The latter is as though a sow wanted to instruct Minerva." And on the left: "I had already decided yesterday and even before that I would not allow you to copy anything for me any more." And at the right: "You should do Mozart and Haydn the honor of not abusing their names in this sort of thing." (Beethovenhaus, Bonn)

BEETHOVEN AND YOUNG LISZT

Liszt had come to Vienna for the completion of his studies and was taught piano by Czerny, and harmony and composition by Salieri. Liszt and his father attempted in vain, and several times, to make Beethoven's acquaintance. Only when Liszt played a concert in Vienna was it possible for him to meet the old master.

FRANZ LISZT IN 1824

Lithograph by Villain after a drawing by A. X. Leprince
(Collection R. Bory)

PROGRAM GIVEN BY LISZT IN VIENNA APRIL 13, 1823

Beethoven, enthusiastic about the great artistry of the virtuoso who was then eleven, embraced him. (National Museum, Budapest)

LUDWIG VAN BEETHOVEN EMBRACING FRANZ LISZT
DURING THE CONCERT OF APRIL 13, 1823

After a lithograph, unsigned, which was published in Budapest in 1873 on the occasion of the Franz Liszt Jubilee. Beethoven generally thought little of young virtuosos and only at the instigation of Schindler had attended this concert. Schindler had heard the prodigy previous to the concert and called his immense talent to Beethoven's attention. (Collection R. Bory)

MISSA SOLEMNIS

The composition on this Solemn Mass had begun in 1819 but was completed only in 1823. Originally it was supposed to have been performed in March, 1820 on the occasion of Archduke Rudolf's consecration as Cardinal Archbishop of Olmütz. However, only on March 23, 1823 did Beethoven present the Mass to his patron, the Archduke. To him the work is dedicated despite the belated completion. On May 7, 1824 the Kyrie, Credo and Agnus Dei were performed in Vienna. That date also signifies the first performance of the Ninth Symphony.

MANUSCRIPT AUTOGRAPH OF THE FIRST PAGE OF THE KYRIE OF THE MISSA SOLEMNIS, OPUS 123

At the head of the autograph Beethoven has written, in his own hand, "coming from the heart may it return to the heart." (Former State Library, Berlin)

THE NINTH SYMPHONY

Even before the year 1817 one can find in Beethoven's sketchbooks certain notes pertaining to the Ninth Symphony. They prove the long period of time over which the work originated. In 1822 and 1823 the various studies led to the chief work of the composer, the D minor Symphony, No. 9, with the final chorus on the Schiller "Ode to Joy."

MANUSCRIPT
OF THE NINTH SYMPHONY, OPUS 125
Title page with the dedication to Frederick William III, King of Prussia

In the autograph of the Ninth Symphony the title page is missing. Beethoven wrote the dedication reproduced here at the head of the score manuscript, which is by the hand of Peter Gläser, the copyist. The dedication addresses itself to the King of Prussia. (Former State Library, Berlin)

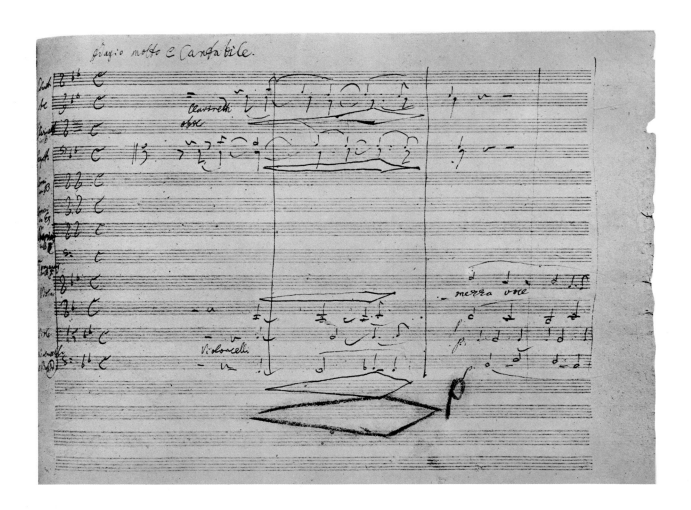

A PAGE FROM THE AUTOGRAPH OF THE NINTH SYMPHONY

Beginning of the Adagio molto e cantabile. (Former State Library, Berlin)

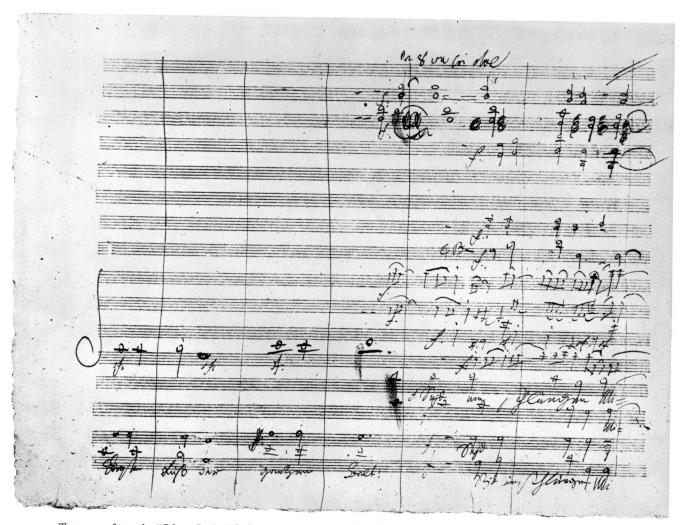

Two pages from the "Ode to Joy" with the famous passage: "Be embraced millions — — this kiss to the whole world."

The obstacles which presented themselves before the concert in which for the first time parts of the Missa Solemnis and the Ninth Symphony were to be performed seemed hardly surmountable. At any rate, the Viennese public was close to having to renounce this great musical event in favor of the Berlin audiences.

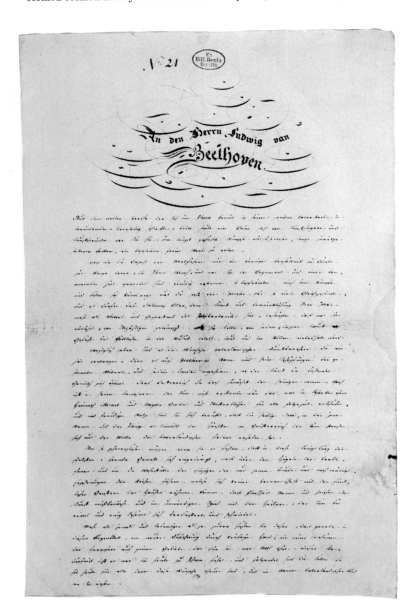

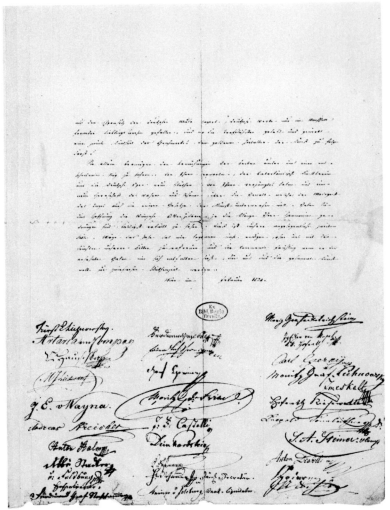

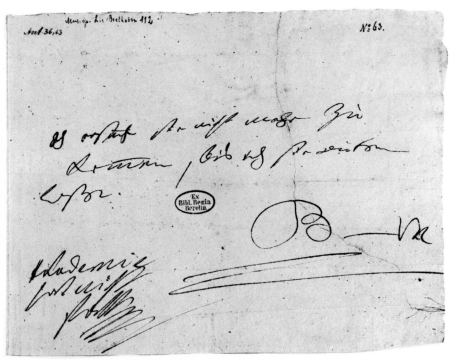

THE FIRST AND LAST PAGE OF THE "PLEA" ADDRESSED TO BEETHOVEN IN FEBRUARY, 1824 BY ARTISTS AND MUSIC LOVERS OF VIENNA

The tremendous successes of Italian operas, and particularly of those by Rossini, in Vienna and moreover the almost complete indifference of the Viennese population to German music had so disgusted and discouraged Beethoven that he isolated himself increasingly, avoided the public and began to distrust even his most faithful friends. This inclination was aided by his natural timidity and by the deafness which at this time was almost complete. When his admirers learned that Beethoven was seriously considering offers from Berlin, they addressed the "Plea" to him and begged him to give the honor of a first performance of the Ninth Symphony and the Missa Solemnis to the City of Vienna. (Former State Library, Berlin)

NOTE OF BEETHOVEN TO SCHINDLER

Beethoven's friends with great effort had succeeded in persuading him to prepare a big concert in Vienna in which the Mass and the Ninth were to be performed. Beethoven, however, convinced that such a concert would be a disaster and that a conspiracy against him was under way, made the enterprise twice as difficult. One day he believed that Prince Lichnowsky, Schuppanzigh and Schindler had betrayed him and sent three insulting notes to these most faithful protagonists. To Schuppanzigh he wrote: "Don't pay me any more visits. I give no more concerts. Beethoven." The note to Schindler said furiously: "Don't call on me until I ask you to. The Academy is not forthcoming. Beethoven." Prince Lichnowsky, his old patron, received a letter with the words: "I am contemptuous of falsities. Don't visit me any more. The concert will not take place. Beethoven." (Former State Library, Berlin)

Große musikalische Akademie
des Herrn
Ludwig van Beethoven
den 7. May im k. k. Hoftheater nächst dem Kärntnerthore
zu seinem Vortheile.

Die dabey vorkommenden Musikstücke sind die neuesten Werke des
Herrn van Beethoven.

1) Große-Ouverture.
2) Drey große Hymnen, mit Solo= und Chorstimmen.
3) Große Symphonie mit im Finale eintretenden Solo= und
Chorstimmen.

Die Dlles. Sontag und Unger und die Herren Haizinger und
Preisinger werden die Soloparten vortragen. Herr van Beetho-
ven selbst wird mit den Herren Umlauf und Schupanzigh das
Ganze leiten.

ANNOUNCEMENT OF THE CONCERT OF MAY 7, 1824 IN VIENNA
(Beethovenhaus, Bonn)

PROGRAM OF MAY 7, 1824

After numerous excitements the day approached on the evening of which the
memorable concert took place in the hall of the Kärntnerthor Theater. After the
Overture for Large Orchestra, opus 124, the Viennese audiences heard the Kyrie,
the Credo and the Agnus from the Missa and, at the end, and as the apotheosis, so
to speak, of it all, they heard the Ninth Symphony. (Former State Library, Berlin)

**Große
musikalische Akademie**
von
Herrn L. van Beethoven,
welche
morgen am 7. May 1824,
im k. k. Hoftheater nächst dem Kärnthnerthore,
abgehalten wird.

Die dabey vorkommenden Musikstücke sind die neuesten Werke
des Herrn Ludwig van Beethoven.

Erstens. Große Ouverture.

Zweytens. Drey große Hymnen, mit Solo- und Chor-
Stimmen.

Drittens. Große-Symphonie, mit im Finale eintretenden Solo- und Chor-Stimmen, auf Schillers Lied, an
die Freude.

Die Solo-Stimmen werden die Dlles. Sontag und Unger, und die Herren Haizinger und Seipelt vortragen.
Herr Schuppanzigh hat die Direction des Orchesters,
Herr Kapellmeister Umlauf die Leitung des Ganzen, und
der Musik-Verein die Verstärkung des Chors und Orchesters aus Gefälligkeit übernommen.

**Herr Ludwig van Beethoven selbst, wird an
der Leitung des Ganzen Antheil nehmen.**

Die Eintrittspreise sind wie gewöhnlich.

Die Logen und gesperrten Sitze sind am Tage der Vorstellung
an der Theaterkasse, in der Kärnthnerstraße Nro. 1038, im Eckhause
beym Kärntnerthore, im ersten Stocke, zu den gewöhnlichen Amtsstunden
zu haben.

Freybillete sind ungültig.
Der Anfang ist um 7 Uhr Abends.

THE KÄRNTNERTHOR THEATER IN VIENNA
Colored engraving by Tranquillo Mollo

The famous concert of May 7, 1824 took place in this theater. Its success was extraordinary. Therefore it was repeated on May 23rd, but at
that time was given in the large Redoutensaal of the Hofburg. (Historical Museum of the City of Vienna)

HENRIETTE SONTAG (1806—1854)

After a lithograph

The celebrated prima donna during the spring of 1824 was in Vienna and sang the soprano part in the first performance of the Ninth. (Opera Library, Paris)

CAROLINE UNGER-SABATIER (1803—1877)

Lithograph by F. von Lütgendorf

She had encouraged Beethoven to give the concert of May 7th. She herself—a singer of great reputation—offered to sing the alto part in the Ninth. (National Library, Vienna)

IGNAZ SCHUPPANZIGH (1776—1830)

Lithograph by Rolling after J. Danhauser

He was the concertmaster during the first performance of the Ninth Symphony. (Historical Museum of the City of Vienna)

ANTON HAIZINGER (1796—1869)

Oil portrait, unsigned

He was the Florestan of the "Fidelio" of 1822 and also participated in the first performance of the Ninth Symphony. (Historical Museum of the City of Vienna)

— 12 —

es in der Musik, wie in der Malerei, verschiedene Schulen, und wie wären solche wohl zu bestimmen? von G. C. F. Lobedanz. — Nachricht für Fr. Rochlitzens Freunde, von d. Red. — Über Wiegenlieder, von St. Schütze. — Reflexionen, von E. Fr. Ebers. — Auflösungen der contrapunctischen Aufgabe: einen Canon zu einem gegebenen Chorale zu setzen: Bearbeitungen von Ant. Reicha, von D. Jelensperger, von Chr. H. Rinck, von F. Kessler, von Zeuner, von Luigi da Niente, von Horstig, von Schnyder von Wartensee nebst Bemerkungen darüber, Bearbeitung von C. Oesterreich, nochmalige von Chr. H. Rinck. —

Intelligenzblatt, Nr. 1 bis 8.

Einladung
zur
Subscription
auf die
drei neuesten grossen Werke
von
L. van Beethoven,
nämlich:
1. Missa solennis, D-dur,
2. Grosse Ouvertüre, C-dur, und
3. Sinfonie mit Chören.
Mainz, bei Schott.

Der Genius der Harmonie ist unserer Zeit besonders günstig. Kaum erlischt ein glänzender Stern am musikalischen Himmel, kaum verstummen die Töne eines geistreichen Compositeurs, so ergänzt ein anderes Genie, den beklagten Verlust zu ersetzen. Mozart und Haydn schwanden, da gab uns die Vorsicht einen Beethoven, der an ihre unsterblichen Werke die seinigen anreiht, völlig würdig, an ihrer Seite die Bewunderung zu theilen. Die Originalität seiner Harmonie, das Liebliche und Ansprechende seiner Modulationen ist unübertreffbar und fliesst rein aus der Fülle eines reichen Genies.

Die unterzeichnete Musikhandlung ist hocherfreut, den Freunden der Kunst den lange ersehnten Genuss der vortrefflichsten seiner Compositionen darbieten zu können.

— 13 —

Diese viel bewunderten Werke erscheinen in nachstehenden Formen:

1. Die grosse Missa solennis
a) in vollständiger Partitur,
b) in ausgesetzten Orchester- und Singstimmen, und
c) im Clavier-Auszuge mit Singstimmen.

2. Die Ouvertüre für grosses Orchester
d) in Partitur,
e) in Orchester-Stimmen.

3. Die grosse Sinfonie mit Chören und Solo-Stimmen (über Shillers „Lied an die Freude")
f) in Partitur,
g) in Orchester- und Singstimmen,
Alles mit dazu gehörigen Verdoppelungs-Stimmen.

Das Ganze wird noch im Laufe dieses Jahres ausgegeben. Die Verleger werden es als eine ihrer schönsten Pflichten ansehen, solche köstliche Werke äusserst correct und in schönem Notenstich auf schönem Papiere, hervorgehen zu lassen.

Um dem Publicum die Anschaffung dieser harmonischen Schätze möglichst zu erleichtern, wird der Weg der Subscription eröffnet, und zwar unter folgenden Bedingnissen:

Es kann nach Belieben auf alle Werke zusammen, also auf die ganze Auflage, subscribirt werden, oder auch nur auf Eines oder einige derselben; z. B. blos auf die Partitur der Messe, ohne die Auflegestimmen, — oder blos auf diese ohne jene, oder blos auf den Clavierauszug, u. s. w.

Da die Bogenzahl noch nicht genau angegeben werden kann, so wird nur im Allgemeinen festgesetzt, dass der gedruckte Bogen nicht über zehn Kreuzer rheinisch kosten wird.

Nach Verlauf der Unterzeichnungsfrist, welche bis Ende Octobers d. J. offen bleibt, wird ein bedeutend erhöhter Ladenpreis eintreten.

Man kann in jeder soliden Buch- oder Musikhandlung subscribiren.

Man bittet, Namen und Wohnort deutlich und unzweideutig zu schreiben, weil das Verzeichnis der resp. Subscribenten den Werken vorgedruckt werden soll.

Mainz, am 20. April 1825.
B. Schott's Söhne,
Grossherzogl. Hof-Musikhandlung.

INVITATION TO THE SUBSCRIPTION PUBLISHED THE 20TH OF APRIL, 1825 IN VOLUME 3, NO. 9 OF THE "INTELLIGENCER OF CÄCILIA" PUBLISHED BY SCHOTT IN MAINZ

This invitation promised a publication of the Missa, the Ninth and "The Consecration of the House" in the near future. (National Library, Vienna)

SUBSCRIBENTEN-VERZEICHNISS
AUF FOLGENDE WERKE
VON
Ludwig van Beethoven.

Missa solennis . . . . . Op. 123.
Ouverture . . . . . . Op. 124.
Sinfonie mit Chor . . . . Op. 125.

Se. Majestät der Kaiser von Russland.
Se. Majestät der König von Preussen.
Se. Majestät der König von Frankreich.
Se. Majestät der König von Dänemark.
Se. Majestät der König von Sachsen.

Se. Königl. Hoheit der Grosherzog von Toscana.
Se. Königl. Hoheit der Grosherzog von Hessen und bei Rhein.
Se. Durchlaucht der Fürst Nicolaus von Galitzin, Obristlieutenant der Russisch Kaiserl. Garde.
Se. Durchlaucht der Fürst Radzivill.

Aachen.
Herren Forstmann, Friedrich Wilhelm.
- Startz, Gotthard.
Amsterdam.
- Hagenaar, L. et J. A.
- Miller, Julius.
- Nolting, J. B.
- Steup, H. C.
Ansbach.
Scherfer, Stadt- und Stiftscantor.
Augsburg.
- Gitter, A.
- Gombart, W.
- Witzka, C. B., Capellmeist. im Dom.
Baden, Canton Aargau.
- Elster, D., Doctor.
Bamberg.
- Lachmüller, J. B.
Barmen.
- Glaeser, Carl.
Basel.
- Neukirch.
Bensheim.
Die Pfarrkirche.
Berlin.
Herren Grochenschütz et Seiler.
- Ideler, K Inspector am Joachimsthalschen Gymnasium.
- Laue, Friedrich.
- Lischke, F. S.
- Merz, Carl, Musiclehrer.
- Moeser, C., Musicdirector.
Schlesinger'sche Buch- und Musikhandlung.
Herren Trautwein, F.
- Wustrow, Hofrath.
Bieberich.
- Rummel, Christian, Musicdirector.
Bologna.
- Cipriani, Musicverleger.
Bonn.
- Simrock, N.
Brandenburg.
- Wiesike, J. J.

Braunschweig.
Herren Hasenbalg, Musicdirector.
- Herrig, C. G.
- Spehr, J. P., Musical. Magazin.
Bremen.
- Stock, J. G.
Breslau.
- Berner, Oberorganist.
- Eppstein.
- Foerster, Carl Gustav.
- Leukart, F. E. C.
- Schnabel, Capellmeister.
- Winterfeld, von, Oberlandesgerichtsrath.
Brottroda, bei Schmalkalden.
- Fuchs, El. Christian, Kaufmann.
Brügge.
- Weber, Musicdirector.
Brünn.
- Gastl, Joh. Georg.
Büren.
- Honcamp, F., Musiclehrer im Seminar.
Carlsruhe.
- Velten, Johann.
Cassel.
- Fischer, J. N., Musicmeister im ersten Linien-Infant. Regiment Churprinz von Hessen.
- Grosheim, Dr.
- Hornthal, Ad.
Chur.
- Tscharner, P. C. von, Obristlieutenant und Director der fahrenden Posten des Cantons Graubündten.
Coblenz.
- Anschütz, Obergerichtsrath.
- Falkenberg, C. J.
- Hoelscher, H. J.
Cöln.
- Almenraeder, Gebrüder.
- Verkenius, Landgerichtsrath.

Constanz.
Herren Seemüller, J. N.
Coppenhagen.
- Loose, C. C.
Danzig.
- Reichel, C. A.
Darmstadt.
Die grossherzogliche Hofcapelle.
Dresden.
Die Arnold'sche Kunst- und Buchhandlung.
Düsseldorf.
Herren Beyer et Comp. G. H.
Elberfeld.
- Bluyssen, P. J.
- Wortmann, Wilhelm.
Erfurt.
- Suppus, J.
Flensburg.
- Korte Jessen.
Frankfurt a. M.
Der Caecilien-Verein.
Herren Gayl, Conrad.
- Guhr, Capellmeister.
- Hedler, G. H.
- Kessler, Ferdinand.
- Scheible, Joh. Nepomuc.
- Stoepel, Doctor.
Freyberg.
- Anacker, Mag., Cantor am Gymnas.
Freyburg.
Die Herder'sche Buchhandlung.
Fulda.
Herren Henkel, M., Musicdirector.
St. Gallen.
- Huber et Comp.
Gebweiler im Elsass.
- Kienzl, Carl, Organist und Musicdirector.
Gend.
- Devylder, A. F.

FIRST PAGE OF THE SUBSCRIPTION LIST PRINTED PRECEDING THE BEGINNING OF THE ORCHESTRAL SCORE OF THE NINTH SYMPHONY

The publisher Schott proudly started the list with the names of the Emperor of Russia and the Kings of Prussia, France, Denmark and Saxony. Then follow the Grand Dukes of Tuscany and Hesse, and then the Princes Radziwill and Galitzin. This list is several pages long. (Conservatory of Music, Geneva)

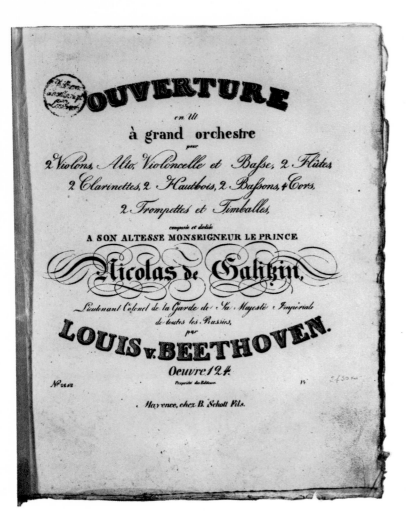

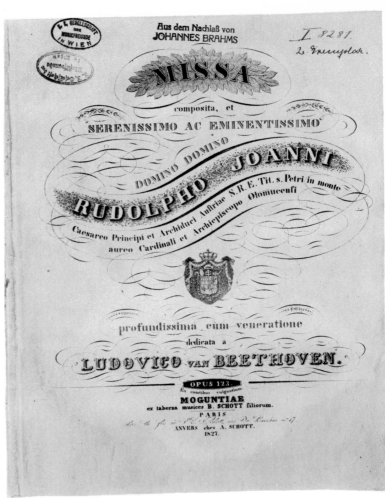

OVERTURE "THE CONSECRATION OF THE HOUSE,"
OPUS 124

Dedicatory page of the score—to the Prince Nikolaus Galitzin

The work was composed in 1822 and published by Schott in Mainz in 1825. (van Hoboken, Ascona)

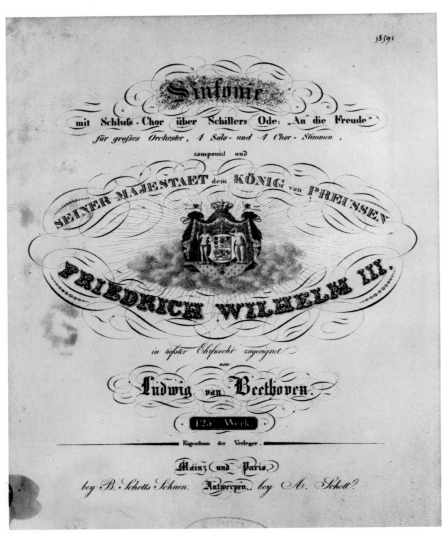

MISSA SOLEMNIS FOR FOUR SOLO PARTS, CHORUS, ORCHESTRA AND ORGAN, OPUS 123

Title page of the score with dedication to Archduke Rudolf of Austria, also Cardinal Archbishop of Olmütz

This copy belonged to Johannes Brahms. The composition was begun in 1819 and completed in 1823. It did not appear in print until 1827, however, published by Schott in Mainz. (Society of Friends of Music, Vienna)

NINTH SYMPHONY, OPUS 125

Title page of the score with dedication to the King of Prussia, Frederick William III

Beethoven's last symphony was published in 1826 by Schott in Mainz. (Conservatory of Music, Geneva)

FRIEDRICH SCHILLER (1759—1805)
Engraving by J. G. Müller after Anton Graff

The great German poet is the author of the "Ode to Joy," the poem on which the final movement of the Ninth Symphony is based. (Former State Library, Berlin)

FREDERICK WILLIAM III, KING OF PRUSSIA (1770—1840)
Engraving by Meno Haas after Lauer

Beethoven had given preference to the King of Prussia over the Emperor of Austria with regard to the dedication of his Ninth Symphony. Was that perhaps the reason why the name of the Emperor of Austria is absent from the list of subscribers to the work? (Former State Library, Berlin)

SEAL ON THE BACK OF A LETTER SENT BY
THE FRENCH EMBASSY OF VIENNA TO BEETHOVEN
(Collection Wegeler, Koblenz)

BOTH SIDES OF A GOLD MEDAL BY GAYRARD SENT BEETHOVEN BY LOUIS XVIII, KING OF FRANCE

When Beethoven was in all sorts of trouble he one day received a message that King Louis XVIII, a most enthusiastic admirer of his, wished to send him a gold medal with the King's likeness on it. Such a distinction was extremely rare and filled the composer with legitimate pride. (Society of Friends of Music, Vienna)

LUDWIG VAN BEETHOVEN
Portrait by Stefan Decker

This portrait was probably created in Beethoven's apartment in 1824.
(Historical Museum of the City of Vienna)

LUDWIG VAN BEETHOVEN (about 1823)

Engraving after a drawing by Martin Tejcek

Contrary to general belief, Beethoven attached great importance to his
wardrobe. Thus Schindler reports that his shirts and collars were always im-
maculately white and that his wardrobe was comprised of a selection of well-
cared-for suits. (Bodmer, Zürich)

LUDWIG VAN BEETHOVEN (1825)
Crayon with water color by Joseph Weidner

Beethoven is shown here from the back and gesticulating
with a cane held in his right hand. (Bodmer, Zürich)

BEETHOVEN WALKING IN THE RAIN
Pen and water color by J. N. Hoechle

Beethoven is seen here during bad weather wrapped in a
raincoat and covering the right side of his face.

LUDWIG VAN BEETHOVEN
SEEN FROM THE BACK
Portrait by Joseph Daniel Böhm

LUDWIG VAN BEETHOVEN
SEEN FROM PROFILE
Portrait by Joseph Daniel Böhm

Both Böhm drawings are probably from the year 1820

LUDWIG VAN BEETHOVEN
After a drawing by J. P. Lyser
(Beethovenhaus, Bonn)

BEETHOVEN IN THE STREETS OF VIENNA
Drawing by J. P. Lyser

Published in 1833 in the periodical Cäcilia in Hamburg, the drawing is accompanied by this caption: "Beethoven is pictured here as he was during the last years of his life when he half-ran and rushed through the streets of Vienna instead of promenading." (Beethovenhaus, Bonn)

LUDWIG VAN BEETHOVEN
Two portraits by J. P. Lyser

It is almost proved that Lyser never saw Beethoven. One is therefore forced to believe that he had at his disposal sketches no longer known today; they served him well for the realization of his later famous drawings. (Private Collection; Society of Friends of Music, Vienna)

KARL, BEETHOVEN'S NEPHEW AND WARD

Karl van Beethoven, Ludwig's younger brother, in Article V of his last will of November 14, 1815, had written thusly: "I make my brother Ludwig van Beethoven the guardian of my son Karl since my greatly beloved brother has helped me so often with truly brotherly love in the most magnanimous and generous fashion that he will in the future transfer the love so often shown me as well as the friendship to my son Karl and that I expect with full confidence and in full reliance on his noble heart; I trust that he will do everything in his power for the mental education of my son and for his further career and I know that my brother will not refuse this my request."

KARL VAN BEETHOVEN AS CADET
(1806—1858)

Portrait, unsigned

When his brother died, Ludwig assumed the guardianship of his nephew Karl. He took these duties most seriously and decided to remove Karl from the bad in-

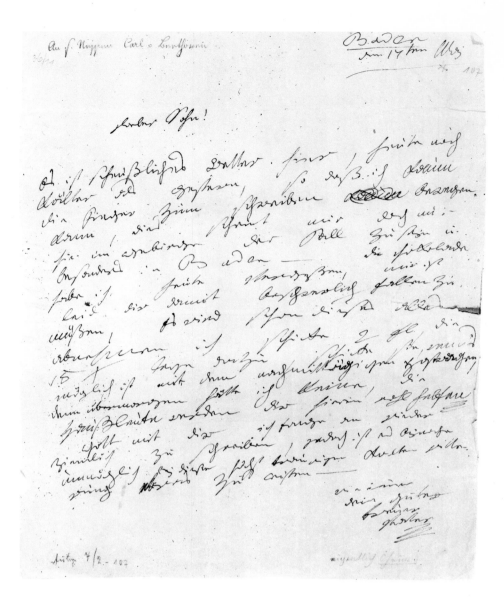

fluences of his mother. He soon regarded him as his own son. In 1817 and 1818 he placed him in the Vienna boarding house Giannatasio del Rio, in 1819 in the Pensionat Blöchlinger. Infuriated over these measures, Karl's mother was so provoked that she started endless suits against her brother-in-law, a cause of greatest sorrow to Beethoven. It is only fair to add that the conduct of the boy was never satisfactory and that the concern of his guardian was fully justified. Beethoven, despite the many inconveniences his nephew caused him, nevertheless retained a passionate affection for him, even though the great sacrifices which he imposed upon himself as the quasi-father were not justified by the boy's behavior. (National Library, Vienna)

A LETTER OF BEETHOVEN TO HIS NEPHEW KARL
(May 17, 1825)

This short letter from Baden begins: "Dear son . . ." and ends with the words: "Your good and faithful father." In the letter Beethoven asks his nephew to send him some chocolate. (National Library, Vienna)

LETTER OF BEETHOVEN TO DR. SMETTANA
(August, 1826)

When his nephew Karl tried to commit suicide Beethoven sent a special delivery letter to the physician: "A great disaster has taken place . . . Karl has a bullet in his head . . . come fast, for heaven's sake, make it fast . . ." (Beethovenhaus, Bonn)

Johann van Beethoven, a young brother of Ludwig (1776—1848)

Portrait by Leopold Gross

In contrast to his older brothers, Johann had succeeded in acquiring a certain fortune. He lived as apothecary for a period in Linz and later bought a farm in Gneixendorf near Vienna. (National Library, Vienna)

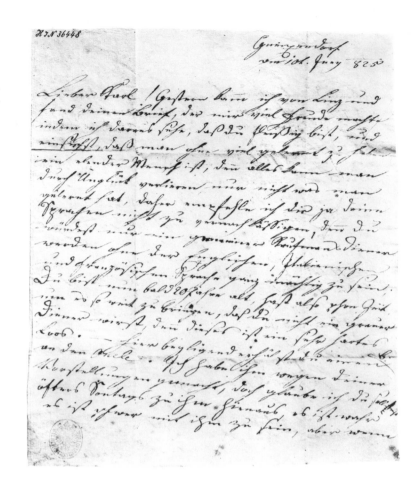

A letter of Johann van Beethoven to his nephew Karl (June 10, 1825)

In this letter he gives his nephew some advice and refers him to all the good things his uncle and guardian Ludwig had done for him. At the beginning of the second page he writes: "If you, however, think of all the things your uncle has already done for you you must realize that he has spent probably in excess of 10,000 florins in your behalf, and what trouble and sorrows have you caused him! When one is young one does not see such things, but you will understand it much better as you get older . . ." (City Library, Vienna)

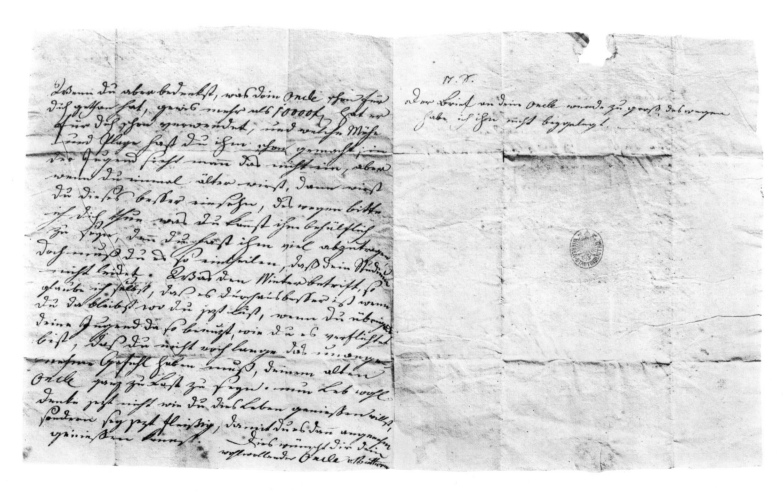

BEETHOVEN IN THE SCHWARZSPANIERHAUS IN VIENNA

During October, 1825 Beethoven established himself in the old monastery of the "Black Spaniards" where he remained—except for two months in the autumn, 1826—to his death in 1827.

CHURCH AND MONASTERY OF THE BLACK SPANIARDS IN VIENNA
Pencil with water color by Ludwig Cserny

Beethoven's apartment in 1825 was on the upper floor of the building near the church at the right of the reproduction. Five windows face the square: that above the main entrance and four facing toward the church. In the building at the left in the reproduction was the apartment of Beethoven's friend Stephan von Breuning with his family—it was in the so-called "Red House." (Collection de Breuning, Paris)

BEETHOVEN'S WRITING DESK

After the composer's death it was acquired by Stephan von Breuning. (Bodmer, Zürich)

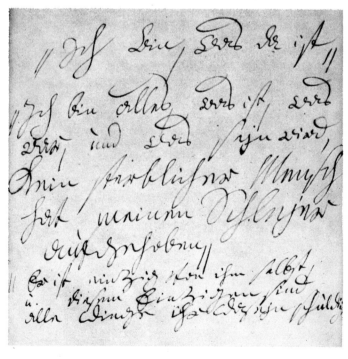

BEETHOVEN'S MOTTOES

"I am what there is. I am everything that is, was and will be. No mortal has lifted my veil." — "He is only by himself and to him alone do all things owe their existence." — The sentences found in an Egyptian temple were copied by Beethoven in a German translation. He had put them up above his desk. (Collection Wegeler, Koblenz)

BEETHOVEN'S STUDY
IN THE SCHWARZSPANIERHAUS
Sepia by J. N. Hoechle

The drawing was made in the study three days
after Beethoven's death. Through the window
one recognizes the steeple of St. Stephan's Cathedral. (Historical Museum of the City of
Vienna)

THE SCHWARZSPANIERHAUS
After an engraving

The former monastery had been secularized
and was the property of the Count Somsich
when Beethoven lived there. It was razed in
1904. (Historical Museum of the City of
Vienna)

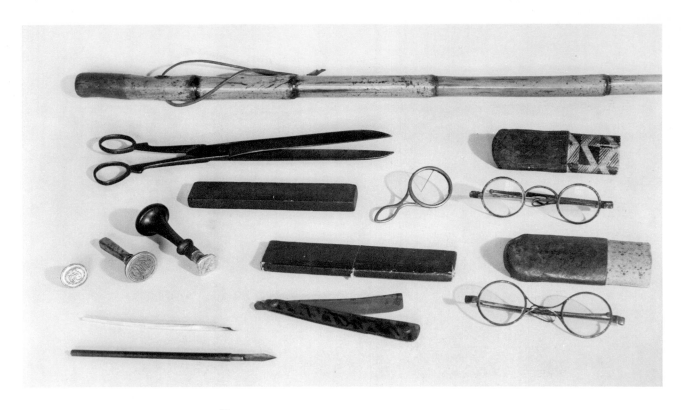

PERSONAL BELONGINGS OF THE COMPOSER

After Beethoven's death Schindler collected and preserved these articles faithfully. When he died they became the property of a collector and later were made part of the collections of the Beethovenhaus. (Beethovenhaus, Bonn)

VARIOUS OBJECTS ON BEETHOVEN'S WRITING DESK

After the death of the master they also came into Schindler's possession: from left to right, a handbell with which he called the domestic; a bronze candle holder with the picture of Amor in a little ship, with a shade; two bronze paper weights showing cossacks on horseback; a bust of Lucius Brutus whom Beethoven greatly revered, and finally, a clock which had been a present of the Princess Lichnowsky. (Beethovenhaus, Bonn)

THE BREUNING FAMILY

Stephan von Breuning was one of the sons of the "Madame Councillor" who had so generously opened her home to Beethoven in Bonn. He had settled in Vienna and had entered the Imperial administration. The old friendship between him and Beethoven, except for temporary disagreements, remained sincere and cordial to the end of Beethoven's life. Indeed, when the composer moved into the Schwarzspanierhaus, their contact became even closer and their friendship greater; Breuning and his family then lived in the former monastery's "Red House."

STEPHAN VON BREUNING AND HIS FAMILY
Painting by an unknown master

Together with the head of the family, his second wife, Constanze, née Ruschowitz, and the children Gerhard, Helene and Maria.
Madame von Breuning aided in Beethoven's household whenever he was in trouble, and was particularly helpful in his sometimes violent quarrels with the personnel. (Collection de Breuning, Paris)

GERHARD VON BREUNING (ca. 1825)
(1813—1892)
After a lithograph

Beethoven had great affection for him, calling him sometimes "Ariel" and sometimes "Pantsbutton." The child spent long hours at the deathbed of the master. In 1874 he published the famous memoirs pertaining to Beethoven's last years in Vienna. The title of the book was "Aus dem Schwarzspanierhaus." (Collection de Breuning, Paris)

STEPHAN VON BREUNING (1774—1827)
After a lithograph

In the autumn of 1805, after the failure of "Fidelio," Breuning changed the libretto for the performances of 1806. He then had his own lyrics distributed during the intermission, and that poetry was composed in Beethoven's honor. Beethoven, in turn, dedicated his opus 61, the Violin Concerto, to him. After the death of his friend Breuning assembled whatever he could acquire from Beethoven's property. (Collection de Breuning, Paris)

THE COMPOSERS OF THE LIGHT MUSE AT THE PRATER

During the years from 1820 to 1825, Joseph Lanner and Johann Strauss the elder, the creators and masters of the Viennese waltz, brought that form to such a perfection that they had the public of the capital on the Danube dancing to their strings. The waltz had sprung up in the café houses of the suburbs and passed from the concert houses at the Prater into the palaces. The waltz brought Johann Strauss the title of Court Kapellmeister.

THE PRATER OF VIENNA
Water color by Karl Schubert, Franz Schubert's brother

The Prater, a very large park, first was the private property of the Imperial family, but in 1766 was opened to the public by Emperor Joseph II. The part of the park closest to the capital gradually became an amusement park, whereas the parterre and the avenues farther south constituted a popular meeting ground for the nobility and the higher middle class. (Private Collection, Vienna)

JOSEPH LANNER (1801—1843)
Lithograph by Joseph Kriehuber

The father of the Viennese waltz had started out with a modest trio, expanded to a quintet and finally to a large orchestra. His successes were incredibly great. Lanner's point of departure was the Ländler in three-quarter time, and gradually he composed his immortal waltzes. (National Library, Vienna)

JOHANN STRAUSS THE ELDER (1804—1849)
Lithograph by Joseph Kriehuber

Strauss originally was a member of the Lanner ensemble. He later left it, formed his own orchestra and celebrated the greatest triumphs. So huge were his successes that he was appointed Court Kapellmeister. (National Library, Vienna)

JOSEPH BÖHM (1795—1876)
Lithograph by Joseph Kriehuber

The excellent musician and violin virtuoso came to the attention of the
Viennese audiences through his excellent performances of Beethoven's
last string quartets. (Historical Museum of the City of Vienna)

THE FIRST CAFÉ HOUSE AT THE PRATER OF VIENNA
Colored engraving by Norbert Bittner

In this large hall the Böhm Quartet played its chamber music matinées for the first time in 1821. Its specialty
was Beethoven's last string quartets. Some of these had their first public performance in the large hall of this
building. (Historical Museum of the City of Vienna)

These quartets are opus 127, 130 and 132. Together with the quartets opus 131, 133 and 135, they are commonly referred to as the "last quartets" of Beethoven. When the composer was in full possession of his artistic means he developed a style entirely his own. However it was that style which also gave him the reputation of having destroyed the forms of tradition.

SKETCH FOR THE STRING QUARTET IN E FLAT MAJOR, OPUS 127

The work was created between 1822 and 1825 and published in 1826. On March 6th, 1825 it was first performed by the Schuppanzigh Quartet. It had no success whatsoever. It was repeated by the Böhm Quartet which played it twice in succession in one and the same concert; at that time it received the enthusiastic acclaim of the audience. The reproduced page is part of the first variation of the second movement. The note at the head of the page is Beethoven's and is directed to an inadequate copyist: "The gentleman need not come back because I cannot use him as a copyist and his stupidity makes everything futile." (Society of Friends of Music, Vienna)

STRING QUARTET, B FLAT MAJOR, OPUS 130

Title page of the score with dedication to Prince Nicolaus Galitzin

Composed in 1825, it was performed for the first time by the Schuppanzigh Quartet on March 21, 1826—in its first version with the final fugue. It was published only after Beethoven's death—in 1827—by Artaria in Vienna. (Society of Friends of Music, Vienna)

AUTOGRAPH OF THE STRING QUARTET IN F MAJOR, OPUS 135

First page of the first movement

Completed in October, 1826 it was published in September, 1827 by Schlesinger in Berlin and Paris. Beethoven had dedicated the work to his friend Johann Nepomuk Wolfmayer. (Bodmer, Zürich)

STRING QUARTET IN C SHARP MINOR, OPUS 131

Title page of the score with the dedication to Baron von Stutterheim

Completed in 1826, it was published by Schott in Mainz in April, 1827. The agreement between the publisher and the composer was signed six days before Beethoven's death (see page 213). (Society of Friends of Music, Vienna)

GREAT FUGUE FOR STRING QUARTET IN B FLAT MAJOR, OPUS 133

Title page of the score with the dedication to the Archduke Rudolf of Austria

Before it became an independent composition, the work had been thought of as the final movement of the string quartet opus 130, for which Beethoven later wrote a different finale. The Fugue was published as an independent work by Artaria in Vienna in 1827. (Society of Friends of Music, Vienna)

In the autumn of 1826 Beethoven had stayed in Gneixendorf. The grief and annoyances with respect to his nephew Karl gave him no respite. On December 2nd he decided to return to Vienna. His health had considerably deteriorated. He required the services of his physician at once. In lieu of the doctors usually taking care of him he sought the advice of Dr. Wawruch, a very conscientious and experienced practitioner who apparently treated pulmonary diseases with success. Unhappily, however, a vomiting spell complicated the situation and was followed by dropsy. This marked the beginning of an agony of more than three months.

DR. ANDREAS IGNAZ WAWRUCH (1772—1842)
Lithograph by F. Wolf

He was a professor at the University of Vienna and treated Beethoven during his last illness. After the death of his illustrious patient he wrote a "Medical review: Beethoven's Last Period of Life," published after Wawruch's death. (Historical Museum of the City of Vienna)

JOHANN SEIBERT
Lithograph by Joseph Kriehuber

Wawruch decided to call this in famous surgeon for consultation. Seibert performed four successive operations on Beethoven which were to free him from suffocating attacks resulting from dropsy. (National Library, Vienna)

JOHANN VON MALFATTI (1775—1859)
Lithograph by Joseph Kriehuber

He won a reputation as a doctor during the Congress of Vienna and treated Beethoven from 1809. The master composed a cantata for him which was first performed on June 24, 1814. Later they had serious disagreements. However, upon the insistence of Schindler, Malfatti consented to treat Beethoven during his last illness, and a touching reconciliation took place at the sickbed. (Historical Museum of the City of Vienna)

NANETTE SCHECHNER-WAAGEN (1806—1860)
Lithograph by Joseph Lanzedelly

This excellent singer was a member of the Vienna Opera to which she had belonged since 1825. She paid Beethoven a visit. When she found him on his sickbed she complied with his wish to sing the great aria of Leonore from "Fidelio" for him. "You certainly are a great artist, and I thank you for this beautiful hour," said Beethoven carried away with joy. (Society of Friends of Music, Vienna)

SKETCHES FOR A SCHERZO TO THE TENTH SYMPHONY

No sooner was the Ninth Symphony completed than Beethoven projected the composition of a Tenth. Since 1825 he had made the sketches for the work which can be found in his notebooks. Suddenly one day when he was again in pressing need of money he received an advance of 100 pounds sterling toward a new symphony, commissioned by the London Philharmonic Society. Notwithstanding his bad state of health, he immediately tried to compose the work. He jotted down a Scherzo, entitling it "Presto." On the following page he wrote the first measures of a fugue on the name *Bach*. The inscriptions are hardly decipherable to the reader but for Beethoven they had a precise meaning. (Former State Library, Berlin)

THE LAST PAGE OF MUSIC WRITTEN BY BEETHOVEN

During the course of his last illness Beethoven incessantly spoke of the music he wanted to compose and which only he, as he said, could compose. He filled his sketchbooks with sketches for a Tenth Symphony. Schindler wrote at the bottom of this page: "These notes are the last ones Beethoven wrote approximately ten to twelve days before his death. He wrote them in my presence." (Former State Library, Berlin)

ANSELM HÜTTENBRENNER (1784—1868)

Lithograph by Joseph Teltscher

Beethoven had met the composer when both were working with Salieri. Theirs was a solid friendship. Salieri saw the composer frequently and Beethoven died during one of Hüttenbrenner's visits on March 26, 1827. (National Library, Vienna)

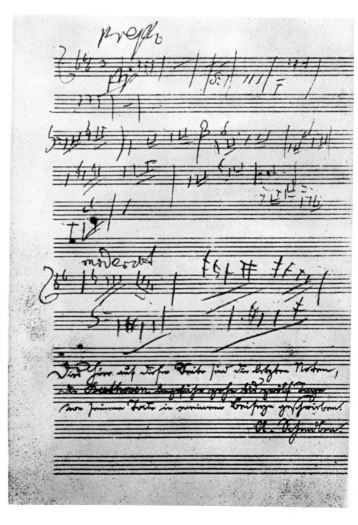

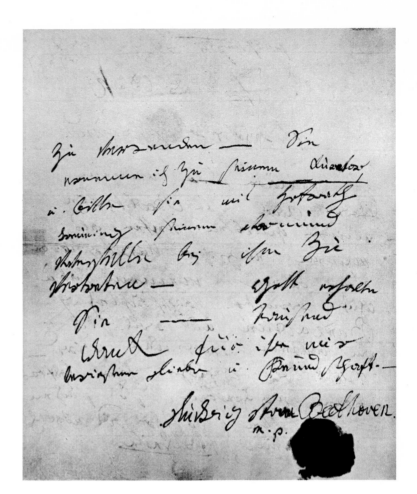

LETTER TESTAMENT OF BEETHOVEN TO HIS VIENNESE ADVOCATE DR. BACH (January 3, 1827)

With this document Beethoven institutes his "beloved nephew Karl" as universal heir. The attorney Johann Baptist Bach was to assume the guardianship of the young man after Beethoven's death. (Municipal Archive, Vienna)

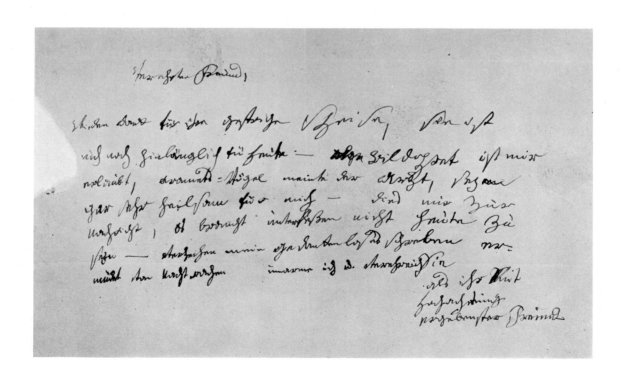

LETTER OF BEETHOVEN TO BARON JOHANN BAPTIST PASQUALATI (March 14, 1827)

His friend Pasqualati was a merchant who had amassed a fortune. He had been Beethoven's counselor in financial and family affairs. Within the period of 1804 to 1814 Beethoven lived, on various occasions, in the Baron's home, Mölkerbastei 8. Beethoven dedicated the "Elegiac Chant," opus 118, to him in memory of his deceased wife. Twelve days before his death—on March 14, 1827—Beethoven sent a letter to Pasqualati thanking him for victuals which the Baron had sent him, and letting him know what he was permitted to eat. (National Library, Vienna)

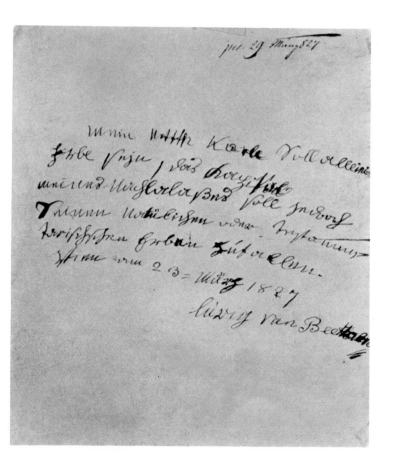

BEETHOVEN'S LAST TESTAMENT (March 23, 1827)

Beethoven, tormented by the destiny of his nephew, through this Testament made
three days before his death proved his generosity toward Karl. He had long
meditated about this affair and communicated his intentions to his brother Johann
and to his friend Breuning. When these two men knew that Beethoven's end was
approaching they, aided by Schindler, put the pen in his hand, so that the
moribund master could sign his last wishes. (Municipal Archive, Vienna)

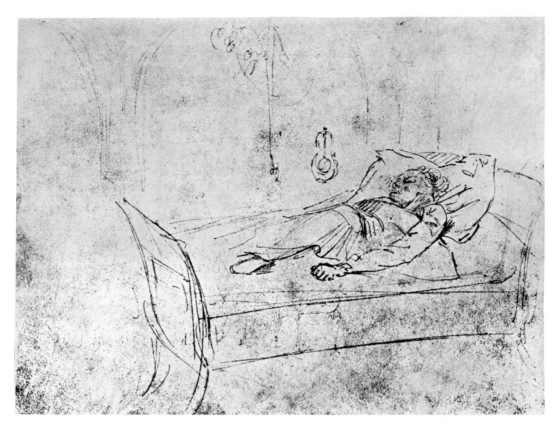

BEETHOVEN IN AGONY
Pencil drawing by Joseph Teltscher

Hiller, who together with his wife had paid Beethoven a visit writes thereafter (March 23, 1827): "The sight of this extraordinary man was horrible . . . he was lying there pale and miserable and at times sighing deeply. No word came from his lips and his forehead was wet with perspiration . . ."

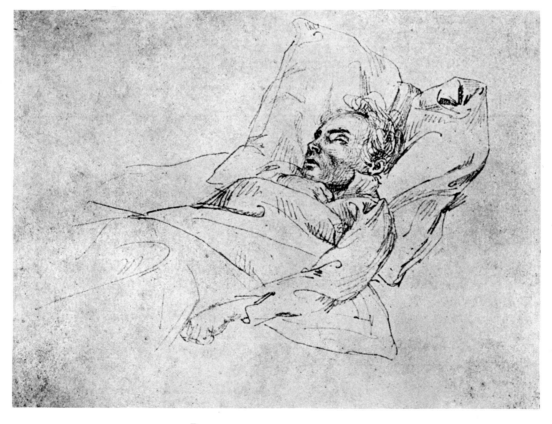

BEETHOVEN ON HIS DEATHBED
Pencil drawing by Joseph Teltscher

On March 24, 1827 the composer, after having received the sacraments, sank into a deep coma. He lived another two days; death came on March 26, 1827 about five o'clock in the afternoon while a tremendous storm was raging over Vienna. Anselm Hüttenbrenner was holding the head of the dying master. The only other person present was his sister-in-law, the wife of Johann van Beethoven. (Both drawings were owned last by Stefan Zweig)

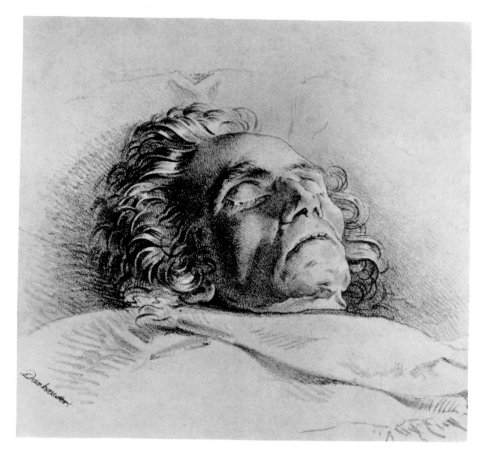

BEETHOVEN ON HIS DEATHBED

Lithograph by Joseph Danhauser after his own drawing

Danhauser, commissioned to take the Beethoven death mask, used that opportunity for the above drawing made on March 28, 1827; at the same time he painted the hands of the deceased. (Historical Museum of the City of Vienna)

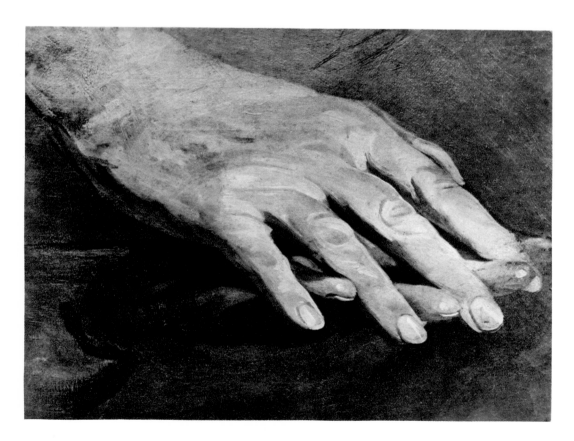

BEETHOVEN'S HANDS

Sketch by Joseph Danhauser

This work was created at Beethoven's deathbed on March 28, 1827. (Historical Museum of the City of Vienna)

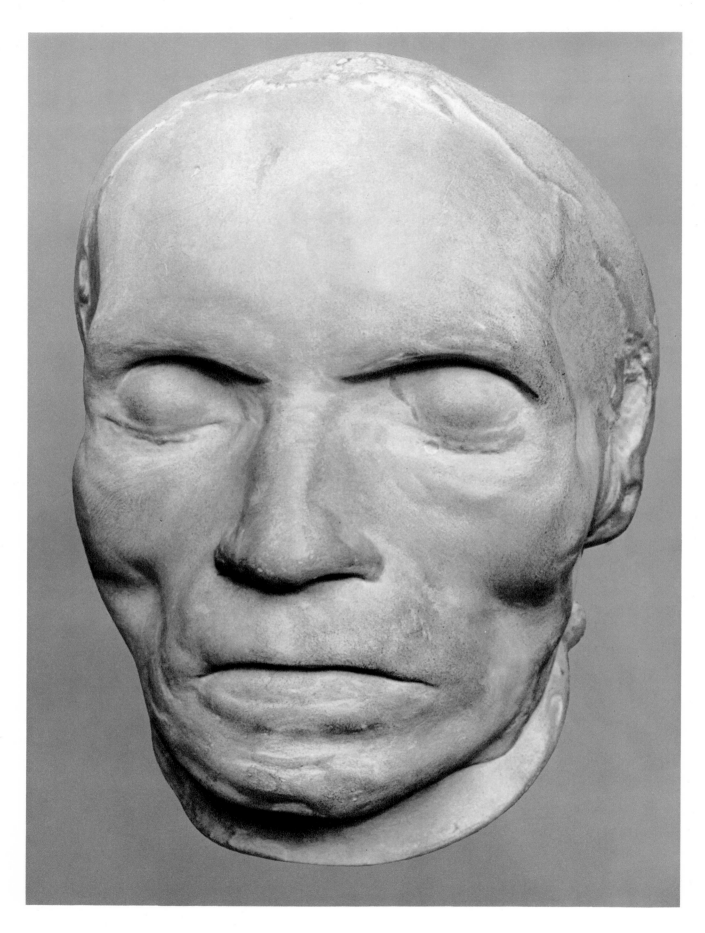

BEETHOVEN'S DEATH MASK

A mold by Joseph Danhauser

Before Danhauser took the death mask on March 28, 1827 the physician in charge of the autopsy had removed the inner and outer ears from the corpse in order to try to establish the causes of Beethoven's deafness. No doubt this surgery had considerably changed his face, already strongly marked by grave illness. (Beethovenhaus, Bonn)

BEETHOVEN'S FUNERAL (March 29, 1827)

Einladung

zu

Ludwig van Beethoven's

Leichenbegängnisse,

welches am 29. März um 3 Uhr Nachmittags Statt finden wird.

Man versammelt sich in der Wohnung des Verstorbenen im Schwarzspanier-Hause Nr. 200,
am Glacis vor dem Schottenthore.

Der Zug begibt sich von da nach der Dreyfaltigkeits-Kirche
bey den P. P. Minoriten in der Alfergasse.

Die musikalische Welt erlitt den unersetzlichen Verlust des berühmten Tondichters am 26. März 1827 Abends gegen 6 Uhr.
Beethoven starb an den Folgen der Wassersucht, im 56. Jahre seines Alters,
nach empfangenen heil. Sacramenten.

Der Tag der Exequien wird nachträglich bekannt gemacht von

L. van Beethoven's
Verehrern und Freunden.

(Diese Karte wird in Tob. Haslingers Musikalienhandlung vertheilt.)

INVITATION TO BEETHOVEN'S FUNERAL

It was formulated by his faithful friend Stephan von Breuning. (Collection Cortot, Lausanne)

THE FUNERAL PROCESSION
Water color by Franz Stöber

The funeral procession began at the Schwarzspanierhaus, in the court of which the first ceremony took place, and led to the church at the Alserstrasse. From there the cortege went to the Währing Cemetery. The estimated number of persons following the hearse was 20,000. (Beethovenhaus, Bonn)

217

MANUSCRIPT OF THE FUNERAL SERMON
AUTHORED BY GRILLPARZER
FOR BEETHOVEN'S ENTOMBMENT

First page of the manuscript. (Municipal Library,
Vienna)

FRANZ GRILLPARZER (1791—1872)

Water color by Moritz Michael Daffinger

The famous Austrian poet was elected to author the
funeral oration. Grillparzer and Beethoven had known
each other since 1805 and had greatest admiration for
one another. (Historical Museum of the City of
Vienna)

HEINRICH ANSCHÜTZ (1785—1865)

Lithograph by Joseph Teltscher

The actor Anschütz, another friend of Beethoven,
delivered the funeral oration authored by Grillparzer.
(Historical Museum of the City of Vienna)

THE AUGUSTINIANS' CHURCH IN VIENNA

After a water color by Joseph Danhauser

On April 3, 1827 a memorial service took place at the Augustinians' Church. The Requiem of Mozart was heard on this occasion with the participation of Italian singers who happened to be present in Vienna for a series of opera performances. Their impresario Barbaja had forbidden these singers to sing at any place other than the theater. The penalty for so doing was 200 guldens. (National Library, Vienna)

LUIGI LABLACHE (1794—1858)

Lithograph of Achille Devéria

Lablache did not mind paying the penalty in order to be able to participate in the homage paid the master. (Opera Library, Paris)

FUNERAL MUSIC FOR BEETHOVEN

This funeral chorus for four parts, men's voices, was composed by Ignaz von Seyfried on words by Jeitteles. The composer used motives from the "Funeral March" of the piano sonata, opus 26 by Beethoven. The work was published by Haslinger in Vienna in June, 1827. (Bodmer, Zürich)

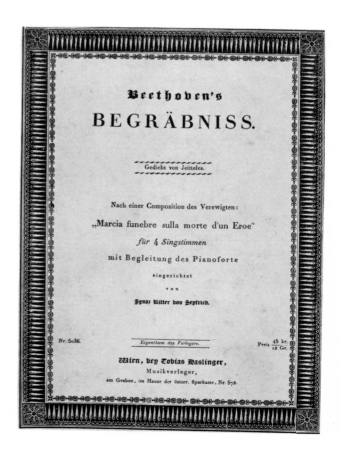

Beethoven's

BEGRÄBNISS.

Gedicht von Jeitteles.

Nach einer Composition des Verewigten:

„Marcia funebre sulla morte d'un Eroe"

für 4 Singstimmen

mit Begleitung des Pianoforte

eingerichtet

von

Ignaz Ritter von Seyfried.

Nr. 5036.   Eigenthum des Verlegers.   Preis 45 kr. 12 Gr.

Wien, bey Tobias Haslinger,
Musikverleger,
am Graben, im Hause der österr. Sparkasse, Nr. 572.

THE WÄHRING CEMETERY IN VIENNA

Steel engraving by M. Aigner after H. Emperger

More than two hundred carriages followed the hearse to the cemetery of Währing. Here, by the grave, the actor Anschütz read the funeral oration penned by Grillparzer. Thereupon Hummel laid a crown on the coffin. A number of mourners took earth from the grave with them. (National Library, Vienna)

TOMBSTONE ON BEETHOVEN'S GRAVE, WÄHRING CEMETERY, VIENNA

Photograph

Beethoven's grave was untouched until 1863 when the corpse was exhumed and his skull was submitted to indiscreet investigations. When they were completed he was buried there for the second time. In 1888 the corpse was again exhumed and Beethoven's remains were transferred to the Central Cemetery of Vienna. At the right of the photograph one recognizes Schubert's grave.

TODAY'S TOMB OF BEETHOVEN, CENTRAL CEMETERY, VIENNA
Photograph

Sixty-one years after his death, in 1888, Beethoven's remains were transferred to this cemetery as was the tombstone erected on his first grave by his friends. (Beethovenhaus, Bonn)

BEETHOVEN'S MONUMENT IN BONN
Work of E. Hähnel after an unsigned lithograph

This Beethoven monument was unveiled in 1845 in the master's native town. It came about as a result of the initiative of a committee headed by Franz Liszt and furthered by him in the most generous manner. (Beethovenhaus, Bonn)

NOTICE TO HEIRS AND CREDITORS OF BEETHOVEN
(April 17, 1827)
(Municipal Archive, Vienna)

APPRAISAL OF BEETHOVEN'S LIBRARY FOR THE
AUCTION (May 5, 1827)
(Municipal Archive, Vienna)

INVENTORY AND APPRAISAL OF MANUSCRIPTS
BY TOBIAS HASLINGER WITH ENTRY OF PRICES
BID AT THE AUCTION (August 16, 1827)

Artaria and Haslinger, publishers, together with Carl Czerny, were commissioned to appraise the manuscripts of Beethoven as found in his apartment after his death. In the first column at the right the appraisal figures are noted, next to it the bid prices of the auction. — Without commentary here follow a few prices for which Beethoven manuscripts were sold: No. 73, two piano trios, fl. 3.40; No. 89, score of the E flat major piano concerto, fl. 3.45; No. 97, score of the Fourth Symphony, fl. 6.40; No. 105, score of the Fifth Symphony, fl. 6.00; No. 115, score of the C minor Piano Concerto, fl. 4.13; No. 122, score of the Septet, fl. 18.00. (Municipal Archive, Vienna)

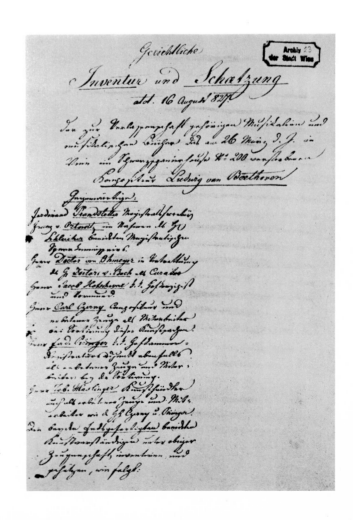

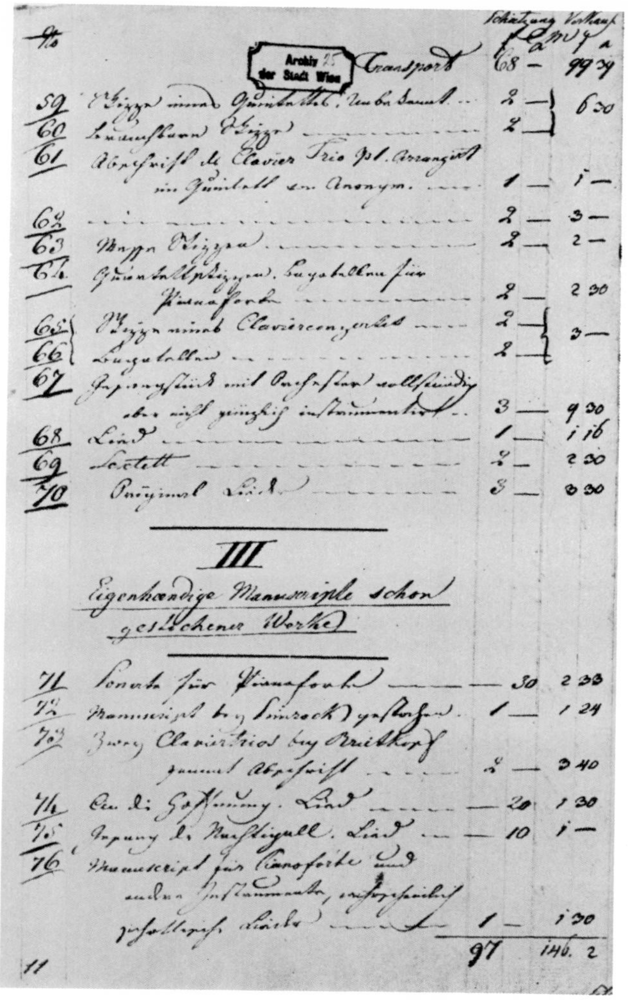

Top left page

No.		Schätzung fl. kr.	Verkauf fl. kr.
	Transport	68 —	99 9
59	Skizze einer Quartett...	2 —	} 6 30
60		2 —	
61	Abschrift des Clavier Trio als arrangirt im Quintett von Anonym	1 —	1 —
62		2 —	3 —
63	Messe Skizze	2 —	2 —
64	Quintettskizzen, eingestellt für Pianoforte	2 —	2 30
65	Skizze eines Clavierconcertes	2 —	} 3 —
66	Bagatellen	2 —	
67	Fugensatz mit Bezifferung vollständig aber nicht gänzlich instrumentirt	3 —	9 30
68	Lied	1 —	1 16
69	Sextett	2 —	2 30
70	Original Lied	3 —	3 30

III
Eigenhändige Manuscripte schon gestochener Werke

No.		Schätzung	Verkauf
71	Sonate für Pianoforte	— 30	2 33
72	Manuscript bey Simrock gestochen	1 —	1 24
73	Zwey Claviertrios bey Breitkopf sammt Abschrift	2 —	3 40
74	An die Hoffnung. Lied	— 20	1 30
75	Opsang d. Nachtigall. Lied	— 10	1 —
76	Manuscript für Pianoforte und andere Instrumente, eingestellt gesellschaftliches Stück	1 —	1 30
11		97 —	146 2

Top right page

No.		Schätzung fl. kr.	Verkauf fl. kr.
	Transport	97 —	146 2
77	Quartettstück, Eg.	— 30	1 —
78	Quartettstück	1 —	3 3
79	Do.	— 30	1 6
80	Finale und die Pastoralsymphonie in Quartett	1 30	2 6
81	sechstes Quartett. 4te Symphonie in Partitur	1 30	5 —
82	für Streich mit den Grossfidelis in Partitur	— 40	2 6
83	Albumblatt	— 30	1 15
84	Fuge im Quartett	— 45	1 40
85	Fantasie Sonate	— 45	2 59
86	Sonate für Clavier und Violin	1 —	1 24
87	Kyrie der ersten Messe in Partitur	1 —	1 40
88	Marsch und fidelis in Partitur	— 40	1 45
89	Clavierconcert in Es Partitur	2 —	3 45
90	Variationen für Pianoforte	1 —	1 30
91	Sonate für Pianoforte u. Violoncello	1 —	2 3
92	Stück Sonate für Pianoforte, nicht vollständig	— 30	36
93	Romanze für Violin. Partitur	— 30	3 41
94	Quartettstück	— 40	52
95	Violinquartettstück, eingeschrieben bey Schuppanzigh	— 5	5 —
96	Ouverture Leonore, mit Bezifferung in Partitur	— 30	24
97	Sinfonia Sinfonie in Partitur	— 4	6 40
98	Schottische Lieder	— 40	1 —
99	Lied	— 10	45
100	Opferlied in Partitur	— 40	1 —
101	Sonate für Pianoforte	1 —	1 30
102	Violinquartettstück	— 5	4 —
103	Christus am Ölberg in Partitur	6 —	7 —
12		134 50	212 10

Bottom left page

No.		Schätzung fl. kr.	Verkauf fl. kr.
	Transport	134 50	212 10
104	Gloria aus der ersten Messe. Partitur	3 —	3 —
105	fünfte Sinfonie in Partitur	5 —	6 —
106	Andante der Pastoralsinfonie. Partitur	3 —	2 53
107	Bagatellen fürs Pianoforte	1 —	3 3
108	Finale des Concertes in Es in Partitur	2 —	2 20
109	Fidelioscenen in Partitur	2 —	2 20
110	Quartett für Violin	2 —	2 20
111	Stück aus Egmont	— 20	50
112	Quartett von Haydn in Partitur geschrieben von Beethoven	— 40	1 —
113	Sinfonie in Partitur	4 —	5 —
114	Fuge von Sebast. Bach im Quartett geschrieben von Beethoven	— 30	40
115	Concert für Pianoforte C dur Part.	3 —	4 13
116	Sonate fürs Pianoforte in As.	1 —	2 —
117	Kuriosstück zu einem Quartett	— 45	1 36
118	Finale des Quartettes in Cis moll	1 —	1 20
119	Quartettstück	2 —	3 —
120	Skizzen zu einer Claviersonate	1 —	2 5
121	Variationen für Clavier	1 20	2 —
122	Originalpartitur des Septettes	3 —	16 —
123	Quartettstück	— 40	1 —
124	Sonate fürs Pianoforte und Flöte	1 —	1 30
125	Zweytes Clavierconcert in Partitur	3 —	4 —
126	Letzte Messe in Partitur	6 —	7 —
127	Quartettstück	— 40	1 —
128	Lied an Chloe	— 30	1 6
129	Zwey Stück aus der Oper Leonore. Partitur	4 —	5 —
3		187 15	295 48

Bottom right page

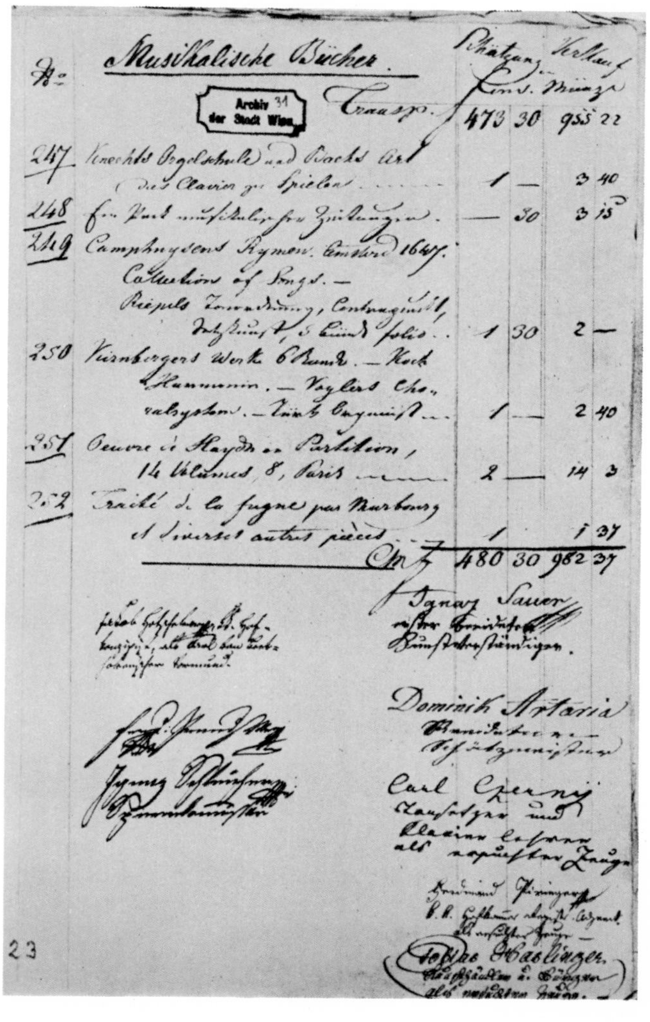

Musikalische Bücher

No.		Schätzung Conv. Münze fl. kr.	Verkauf W. W. fl. kr.
	Transport	473 30	955 22
247	Knechts Orgelschule und Bachs Art das Clavier zu spielen	1 —	3 40
248	Ein Band musikalischer Zeitungen	— 30	3 15
249	Campheysons Rymes. Lond. 1647. Collection of Songs. — Reicha's Zusammenstellung, Contrapunct, dazu 3 Bände u. 3 Hefte folio	1 30	2 —
250	Nürnbergers Werk 6 Bände. — Hoch Glaremein. — Vogler's Choralgesangen. — Dürre's Gesang.	1 —	2 40
251	Oeuvre de Haydn en Partition, 14 Volumes, 8. Paris	2 —	14 3
252	Traité de la fugue par Marpurg et diverses autres pièces	1 —	1 27
	Summe	480 30	982 27

(signatures)

Ignaz Sauer
erster Brei[...]

Dominik Artaria
Buchh[ändler]
Schätzungsmeister

Carl Czerny
Clavierlehrer und Clavier[...]
als angestellter Zeuge

Tobias Haslinger
[...]

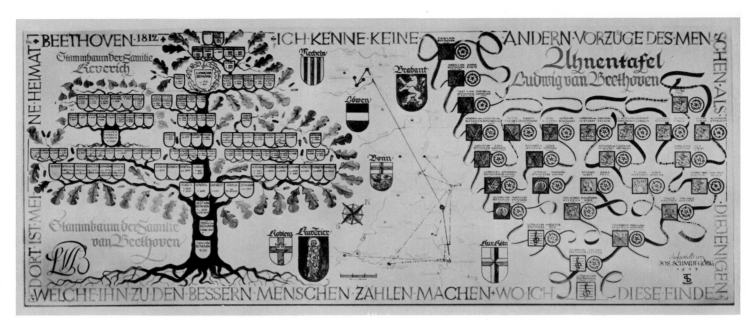

THE BEETHOVEN FAMILY TREES

This double family tree was made after the data provided by Joseph Schmidt-Görg, the present director of the Beethoven Archive and of the Beethoven-haus in Bonn. The panel decorates the vestibule of the Museum.

FRONT OF THE BEETHOVENHAUS IN BONN WITH ENTRANCE TO THE MUSEUM

VESTIBULE WITH STAIRWAY, BEETHOVENHAUS, BONN

EXHIBITION ROOMS IN THE BEETHOVENHAUS, BONN

A QUINTET OF STRINGS

In 1800 Prince Lichnowsky gave Beethoven a gift of a quartet of strings consisting of an Amati violin of 1690; a second violin by Guarneri of Cremona, 1718; a viola made by Vincenzo Rugero detto il Per, Cremona, 1690, and a cello by Andrea Guarneri, Cremona, 1675. Schuppanzigh and his ensemble played Beethoven's quartets on these instruments. In the same glass case in which these are exhibited we see the viola which Beethoven played from 1786 to 1792, that is, before he left Bonn. (Beethoven-haus, Bonn)

AN ERARD PIANO OWNED BY BEETHOVEN

Prince Lichnowsky had ordered two pianos from Erard in Paris (1803), one of which was a present to Beethoven. Beethoven was not completely satisfied with this precious instrument, since even at that time he dreamed of instruments which would have the capacity to express more adequately and more sensitively the musical tempests he could release. There are only three pianos in existence which were Beethoven's property without doubt: in addition to this Erard, the two instruments by Broadwood and Graf. (Collection of the Museum of Linz, exhibited at the Art Museum of Vienna)

Piano from the workshop of Thomas Broadwood
After an unsigned drawing

In 1818 Beethoven received a beautiful instrument from the English manufacturer Thomas Broadwood of London. The beauty of its sound and the extraordinary technical possibilities inherent in the workmanship gave the recipient extraordinary joy. He turned his Erard over to his brother Johann and played only the Broadwood which, to his dying day, was his most faithful friend. Subsequently the piano became the property of Franz Liszt. (National Museum, Budapest)

Piano from the workshop of Konrad Graf, Vienna

When the Broadwood showed signs of deterioration due to daily use and the incessant demands made on it by its owner, Konrad Graf, a Viennese manufacturer of pianos, offered the master one of his instruments. It was put end to end with the Broadwood in Beethoven's room where it remained throughout his life. Graf bought it back from the estate. (Beethovenhaus, Bonn)

LUDWIG VAN BEETHOVEN
Medallion in clay by E. Gatteaux
1827, after the death of the master.

LUDWIG VAN BEETHOVEN
Medallion in silver by E. Gatteaux
1827, after the death of the master. (Society of
Friends of Music, Vienna)

LUDWIG VAN BEETHOVEN
Medallion in bronze by G. Radnitzky

This medallion was made in 1870 (on the occasion of the Beethoven centennial) after the medallion by Böhm of 1822. (Beethovenhaus, Bonn)

LUDWIG VAN BEETHOVEN
Medallion in plaster by Leopold Heuberger

It was created in 1827 after the death of Beethoven. (Historical Museum of the City of Vienna)

LUDWIG VAN BEETHOVEN
Bust in plaster by Joseph Danhauser

The bust is lifesize and was made after Beethoven's death. It seems inspired more by the mask of 1812 than by Danhauser's own mask, the death mask, of 1827. The bust pictured above has particular value because the artist knew Beethoven personally. (Beethovenhaus, Bonn)

INDEX

REGISTER (NAMES)

Names in italics represent those of artists whose paintings, drawings, engravings, etc. are reproduced in this work. A number in parenthesis indicates that several works of the same artist appear on the page referred to or that several reproductions concern the same person, locale or subject matter.

REGISTER

LOCALES

WORK LIST

"K.WoO" means: *Kinsky. Work without opus number*. The subsequent number refers to the numbering in Kinsky's "Thematisch-Biblio-graphisches Verzeichnis aller vollendeten Werke Ludwig van Beethovens" (List of all completed works of Ludwig van Beethoven).